TEACH YOURSELF

HEALTHY

EATING

for

BABIES AND CHILDREN

Mary Whiti̶ng and Ti̶m Lobstein

FOOD
COMMISSION

Publisher of The Food Magazine

Hodder & Stoughton

A MEMBER OF THE HODDER HEADLINE GROUP

Cover photograph Bubbles/Loisjoy Thurston

British Library Cataloguing in Publication Data
A catalogue record for this title is available from The British Library

ISBN 0 340 62706 9

First published 1995
Impression number   10 9 8   7 6   5 4   3 2   1
Year   1999 1998 1997 1996 1995

Typeset by Transet Limited, Coventry, Warwickshire.
Printed in Great Britain for Hodder & Stoughton Educational, a division of
Hodder Headline plc, 338 Euston Road, London NW1 3BH by Cox & Wyman,
Reading, Berkshire.

ACKNOWLEDGEMENTS

There are many people who have helped in large ways to see this book come about, and we want to say an enormous 'thank you' to them all. And we want to say thank you particularly to Helen Strange, the original (highly original) inspiration for this book's predecessor, *The Nursery Food Book* (Edward Arnold, 1992). And thank you particularly to Barbara Crosby, who has read and commented on numerous occasions, always generously and always to our benefit. Our many thanks also to Shelley Lubert, Jean Neal and Vidgis Wold for much help and encouragement, and to Philippa Smith at Eastside Child Care Centre for the use of several of her delicious recipes.

And thank you to our long-suffering and extraordinarily tolerant partners, John Whiting and Kathy Adams.

CONTENTS

PART ONE: A parents' guide to healthy eating

1 Stopping the rot   1
The rot starts early   1

2 Getting ready   4
Preparing for pregnancy   4
Taking the first steps   6

3 Breast or bottle   10
An emotive subject   10
The value of breast milk   12
Formula milks   15

4 Weaning   17
Weaning – the first phase   17
Weaning – the second phase   23
The final phase – six months and onwards   23
Towards family food   24

5 The toddler's good feeding guide   31
Giving them what they want   31

6 Keeping the peace   38
Happy mealtimes   38
Keeping the peace when shopping   43
What do you want for dinner?   44
Visitors bearing gifts   46
A word to grandparents – and others   47
Changing for the better   48

7 Big eaters, small eaters and faddy eaters   52
Coping with rejection   53
Faddiness   59
And big eaters?   62

 8 Food at nursery and playgroup   **64**
       Good nursery ... pity about the food?   64
       Good nursery food   67
       Childminders   71

 9 Cooking with your child   **73**
       Preparing to cook with your children's help!   74
       Kitchen pleasure   75
       Playing with recipes   77

10 Growing food   **86**
       Growing things indoors   87
       Window boxes and tubs   93
       In the garden   95
       Garden safety   101

11 Parties, picnics and outings   **102**
       Setting the scene   102
       Party food ideas   103
       The birthday cake   107
       Drinks   108
       Picnics and outings   108

PART TWO: Recipes
12 Weaning recipes: four to five months old   **113**
       Baby rice   114
       Fruity rice porridge   114
       Pear purée   114
       Apple purée   115
       Carrot purée   115
       Creamy purées   115
       Baby jacket   115
       Banana mash   116
       Banana rice porridge   116
       Papaya   116
       Vegetables from the family pot   116
       Broccoli purée   117
       Cauliflower purée   117
       Broccoli and potato cream   118
       Parsnip purée   118
       Root vegetable purée   118
       Baby beverage   119

       Stage two: five to six months old   **119**
       Avocado pear   119

Fruity avocado   119
Peaches and banana   119
Golden apricot and banana pudding   120
Green beans   120
Leek cream   121
Leeks and green beans   121
Sweet potato   121
Carrot and lentil soup   122

13 Recipes for babies from six to eight months old   123
Baby breakfast cereal   123
Wheatgerm and milk   124
Baby oatmeal   124
Chicken soup   124
Chicken liver purée   126
Liver and tomato dinner   126
Liver, leek and potato dinner   127
Liver, onion and apples   127
Turkey and chestnuts   128
Turkey and winter vegetables   128
Bambino Italiano   129
Fish tasters   129
First fish dinner   130
Baby bubble and squeak   130
Fruity potatoes   130
Fresh fruit yogurt   131
Cooked fruit yogurt   131
Cottage fruit   131

Nine to twelve months old: towards family food   131
Finger foods   132
Brightly coloured vegetables   132
Dips   133
Soft goat's cheese with fruit   134
Baby guacamole   135
Cheese and potato cakes   135
Parsley fish cakes   136
Dairy dinner   137
Bright green cucumbers   137
Spicy swede and carrot   137
Fast fish   138
Midsummer delight   138
Banana whizz   139

14 Family meals   **140**
   Breakfasts   **141**
   Porridge fit for a king   141
   Great granola   141
   Super muesli   142
   Tiny toddlers' breakfast cereals   142
   Creamy scrambled egg   142

   Fish   **142**
   Scottish herring   142
   Trout à la meunière   144
   Mackerel with gooseberry sauce   146
   Mackerel with apricot sauce   147
   Hungarian fish casserole   148
   Fish with cream sauce   149
   Creamless cream sauce   149
   Mushroom sauce   150
   Parsley sauce   150
   Cheese sauce   150

   Pasta   **151**
   Perfect pasta   151
   Pasta with tuna   151
   Peasant pasta   152
   Pasta with bright red and green sauce   152
   Spaghetti Bolognese   153

   Meat and vegetarian dishes   **153**
   Wolf stew   153
   Pizza   154
   Green salad for pizza   156
   Family salad dressing   156
   Italian tomato sauce   156
   Tomato pie   157
   Hurry curry   157
   Brown rice, how to cook   158
   Golden rice for curries   159
   Golden sesame slices   159
   Baby meatballs with dill   160
   Home-made burgers   160
   Beanburgers   161
   Chicken pie   162

Desserts   163
Fresh fruit   163
Winter fruit salad   163
Creamy winter fruit   164
Last minute banana yogurt dessert   165
Strawberry-raspberry dessert   165
Fresh fruit compote   165
Fresh fruit jelly   166
Fresh fruit trifle   166
Strawberry jelly ring   167
Ice-cream pudding with meringues   168
Apricot jelly crunch   169
Raspberry crunch   170
Grandmother Rachel's Polish cheesecake   170

15 **Snacks**   **171**
Breadmaking   171
Sandwiches   175
What to put on toast?   175
Fish pâté   176
Cod's roe pâté   176
Grilled fruit   176
Hot pitta bread   177
Persian hummus   177
Oven chips   177
Kelewele   178
Stir-fried vegetable chips   178
Potatoes-in-their-jackets and fillings   178
Popcorn   179
Lassi   179
Mighty milk shake   179
The sling-in-the-bin list   180
The cut-way-back list   180
Better baking   181

PART THREE: Getting help   **183**
16 **More information, resources and useful addresses**   **185**
People who can help   185
Commercial organisations   186
Support groups   187

Index   **193**
Index to Recipes   **195**

Part One

A PARENTS' GUIDE TO HEALTHY EATING

1
STOPPING THE ROT

The rot starts early

Soft drinks have become so popular among young children that many children never drink water, according to researchers at Southampton University. And a Government survey of school children found that half were eating an average of 150 hamburgers a year each, and the great majority of school children were eating an average 200 portions of chips a year each.

That's an awful lot of soft drinks. And an awful lot of fast food meals. More to the point, it's an awful lot of sugar and fat.

And it appears that the rot starts early. Many baby drinks, being sold as suitable from their first few weeks, are made of little more than sugar and water. They have no useful nutritional value – and worse, they encourage babies to develop a sweet tooth. Baby rusks (still called 'teething' rusks by some) are more sugary than a jam doughnut – and that's the 'low sugar' sort!

As parents we are told that never before have we had such amazing choice. Never before have supermarkets been so stuffed with exotic products and new delightful tastes to try. At the same time, never before have scientists known so much about human nutrition and the needs of babies. So here we have an ideal world, surely?

Well, perhaps not so ideal. Never before have commercial interests been so active and insistent. Never before have there been so many products on the babyfood shelves competing to attract your attention. And never before have we had a population so likely to be overweight, or to visit a doctor because they have adult diabetes. And after a decade of improvement in children's teeth, dentists are finding that tooth decay is on the increase again.

By the time our children reach adulthood the majority will start to suffer the diseases that result from poor diets. We need only look into our own mouths to see the fillings – perhaps not a fatal disease but a costly one, as the dental services cost the NHS over £500 million every year.

If we could look into our hearts and our arteries we might be more alarmed. Heart disease and high blood pressure kill a quarter of us and what we eat contributes greatly to those deaths. Worse still, the age when heart disease strikes is falling – people in their thirties and forties are now having heart attacks in large numbers.

And cancer, the other big killer of the twentieth century, is related to diet. A World Health Organisation report estimates that 40 per cent of cancers in men, and a startling 60 per cent in women, are linked to diets with too much refined, fatty food – especially animal fat – and not enough vegetables and fruit.

From conception to coronaries, cancer to constipation, the food we eat is linked to our health. And it isn't just in adulthood that we should be concerned.

What does this mean for children?

It means a lot! For starters, the habits that children develop will set them up for life. And for seconds, the diseases themselves start early.

Habits learnt young may be the hardest to break. A childhood spent acquiring bad eating habits will increase the chance of a serious disease in adulthood. On present figures, out of one hundred toddlers today, 50 can expect to be medically overweight in adulthood, 40 may die of heart disease (including ten before they reach retirement age) and ten may die of diet-related cancers.

And even in childhood they may start to suffer the consequences of a poor diet. Taking just tooth decay, nearly half of Britain's children will need a filling before their second set of teeth arrive. And nearly three-quarters will have tooth decay in their second set by the age of fifteen.

As for heart disease, the early signs of trouble can be found in the arteries of children as young as one year old. It may be several decades before that artery collapses or blocks up and the consequences of early problems prove to be fatal. But unlike a child's first teeth, an artery does not fall out to be replaced by a new healthy version. Whatever happens to it in the first few years, or even before the baby is born, will affect it for life.

However, don't be alarmed if your child has the occasional chocolate bar or packet of crisps (although stick to the sort without sprayed-on flavourings). Such treats are part of childhood. Just remember to keep them as treats and not for everyday, nor as substitutes for real food. And don't feel too guilty if you find it hard to limit sugary, salty snacks as much as you would like. Remember, manufacturers spend millions on seductive marketing methods designed to make it hard for you – and your child – to resist. On the other hand, you have every right to be *angry* at what you are being sold and the way in which your parental authority is so persistently undermined. Indeed, the way in which commercial interests make parenting increasingly difficult is a subject in itself.

The purpose of this book is to provide a counterblast of information, tips and easy recipes. It's never too late to change things and prevent the rot from getting worse!

2
GETTING READY

Preparing for pregnancy

If you are planning a pregnancy, or are newly pregnant, read this chapter!

How many parents would like to have children who are healthy, intelligent and easy to care for? Who wouldn't! Well, it's not entirely pot luck. Heredity plays a part, but there's also a lot prospective parents can do – if they have the chance to start in good time.

Ideally, that means planning for your baby at least three months before attempting to conceive. Too far back? According to recent research, not a bit! Indeed, if the health of either parent is known to be poor in some way, or if the mother already has a young baby, then six months before might be better.

We are only just beginning to learn how very important the pre-conceptual diet is. We now know that very rapid cell-division begins immediately after conception, and it is because a woman may not know she is pregnant during this crucial time, that preparation for pregnancy is so valuable. Similarly, the health of the father at the time of conception also affects the growth and development of his child.

The first month of pregnancy is the most important. During this time, there is a very high demand for nutrients, as foundations are being laid for the baby's heart, brain and other important organs. Providing these nutrients when they are most needed gives the baby the best start.

Requirements for vitamins B and C are particularly high. Research across several countries has found that many women are not getting enough of these vitamins, even when they appear to be eating well. This is important: for example one of the B vitamins (called folic acid) seems to protect against spina bifida.

> If you can, make an effort to have a really healthy diet before conception and for the first few weeks of pregnancy. The food a pregnant woman eats can influence the health of her child and her grandchild.

There is a strong link between good maternal diet and good birth weight. A poor diet can lead to low birth weight and may raise the chances of the baby showing problems such as blindness, deafness, autism, low IQ, poor speech development, cerebral palsy and health problems in later life such as heart disease, high blood pressure and disorders of the nervous system. But please remember: although a poor diet does increase the chances of these problems and illnesses, a poor diet is not the only cause.

> Do not blame yourself if you have been unable to eat a healthy diet, or if any problem arises later which might have been prevented. This book is not about blaming individuals for what they do. It is about showing how, in small ways, individuals may be able to help prevent problems arising. We, the authors, also believe that there are many ways people should be helped in this regard, for example by ensuring that everyone has access to healthy foods, and enough money to buy such food.

A woman who has produced one bouncing baby with no particular attention to her diet may think she can produce another equally healthy child, again without taking much care over what she eats. She is probably unaware of the many subtle nutritional deficiencies (notably calcium and iron) which the first pregnancy caused her.

These losses should be made good if she is to avoid starting another pregnancy in a depleted state of health. If possible, try to have a gap of at least nine months between one pregnancy and another.

One of the exciting aspects of recent research is that good maternal nutrition is not only the key to good health throughout one baby's life, but that its benefits will also be carried forward to the next generation. What a wonderful opportunity to give the gift of good health to one's children and grandchildren!

As the best way to build up your health is by eating good food, preparing for pregnancy could be rather enjoyable!

Taking the first steps

You may already know, in general terms, what constitutes a good diet. If, however, you haven't got round to actually putting this knowledge into practice, you now have the greatest possible incentive. It may help to write down a sort of battle-plan of all the changes you know you need to make in the way you eat:

1 Write out menus, including any snacks you intend to eat, for the week ahead and shop accordingly. As a reminder, use the 'healthy plate' as a guide (see page 191).
2 Plan to eat a wide variety of foods. A repetitive, narrow diet can produce nutrient deficiencies.
3 Concentrate on nutrient-rich foods. Plan to eat foods that are high in calcium and iron regularly. Also, your need for B vitamins and vitamin E will soar as soon as you are pregnant, so eat foods rich in these. Sufficient calcium is needed for sturdy bones and good teeth.
4 Cut right back on salty and fatty foods, and those which contain a lot of sugar. Remember that ready-prepared foods are often very high in salt, sugar and fat.
5 Compile a list of 'super-special' recipes – perhaps starting with the ones at the back of this book – which are highly nutritious, easy to make and delicious to eat.

In addition:

6 Drop all inessential medication.

7   Remember that smoking and drinking can reduce the ability to conceive and may have a detrimental effect on your baby.

Folic acid deserves a special note. Sometimes referred to as 'folate', it is one of the family of B vitamins and it is found particularly in wheatgerm, nuts, liver, asparagus, pulses and dark green leafy vegetables (hence its name – from 'foliage') and fortified breakfast cereals. Too little folic acid can cause premature birth, miscarriage and birth defects, notably spina bifida. Although it is needed throughout pregnancy, it is especially important during the first few weeks. It is one of the reasons for planning ahead: a mother needs to have rich stores of folic acid so she is ready for the crucial first month of pregnancy.

If you plan to do nothing else to prepare for conception, do at least make sure you have enough folic acid, either by eating plenty of folic-acid-rich foods or by taking a supplement (these can be bought in most shops selling vitamin pills).

Aim to eat around half a milligram or take a supplement of 400 micrograms, just under half a milligram. If you have a history of miscarriages or you have had a baby with spinal tube problems such as spina bifida, then take a higher dose: your GP can advise you on this and may give you a prescription.

All sorts of nutrients are needed throughout pregnancy. Food supplements may help (extra iron and folic acid may be needed), but in general no one should think of pills as any kind of substitute for the array of vitamins, minerals, proteins, phytochemicals (those naturally occurring in plants), essential oils and dietary fibre found in ordinary good food.

What to buy, what to eat

Concentrate on foods high in nutrients: seafood of all kinds, poultry, lean meat, low-fat dairy produce, all kinds of fruits and vegetables, eggs, pulses, wholegrain breads, pasta and rice. Build meals and snacks around these kinds of foods. If you don't eat meat or fish, be sure to eat plenty of nuts, seeds, pulses, eggs, milk, cheese and whole grains.

Don't waste shopping bag (and stomach) space on useless stomach-fillers. Shops are stocked high with all manner of artfully packaged foods and drinks that will contribute virtually nothing to you or your baby's well-being. Worse, many contain high levels of salt, sugar and saturated fat plus a laboratory full of chemical additives which you will both be better off without.

Make a resolution to cut down on commercially made packet pies, cakes, biscuits, instant desserts, soft drinks including most 'fruit' drinks, sugary breakfast cereals, deep-fried foods, salt-laden cocktail snacks and anything containing – or fried in – hydrogenated (artificially hardened) fat. Avoid processed meats and meat products and develop your interest in home cooking; then you will know, for example, how much sugar or salt has gone into the sauces and soups, dressings and desserts.

Caffeine (in tea, coffee, chocolate, and cola drinks) and alcohol both readily enter the baby's bloodstream and should be reduced as much as possible. It is worth noting that tea inhibits the absorption of useful iron.

Eat foods high in fibre such as wholemeal pasta, bread, and brown rice to avoid constipation. Such foods also provide a whole range of invaluable nutrients that are lost when the 'whole' is refined into the 'white'. All fruits, especially figs, fresh or dried, prunes, peaches and strawberries, and all vegetables, especially peas, beans, lentils, parsnips, plantains, potatoes and sweetcorn, are good sources of fibre.

Not all breakfast cereals can be recommended, but shredded wheat is simply wheat that has been shredded, puffed wheat is wheat that has been puffed, and Weetabix is wheat that has been flaked and (with a little sugar added) shaped into biscuits. 'High-bran' cereals can be too high in bran, and anyway tend to have too much sugar or salt added to hide their dull nature. If you want to add bran to your diet (and you shouldn't need to if you are eating whole-grain rather than refined, white versions of bread, pasta, rice, etc.) you can buy packets of plain bran and sprinkle some onto any food you wish.

Beware of commercial 'mueslis': they usually contain lots of added sugar (real muesli contains no such thing) and some kinds contain less fibre than cornflakes! Check the label carefully. Best of all, make your own muesli: it's quickly made and it's cheaper. Try the muesli and granola recipes – on pages 141 and 142.

Liver always used to be recommended as a good food in pregnancy as it is superbly nutritious, but nowadays, because of current farming practices, liver from animals reared on artificial feeds (which contain large amounts of vitamin A) is now far too high in vitamin A to be safely eaten by pregnant women. Liver from free-range animals which have not been fed supplements, however, remains a safe and highly beneficial food. Kidney is a very good alternative.

Four hygiene points

1 Raw vegetables and salads, even if bought as 'ready washed', should be washed in running water to avoid the risk of listeria. Listeria can harm the foetus and cause a miscarriage.
2 Pâté, underdone meat of any kind and soft cheese, such as Camembert and Brie, carry a certain amount of risk of listeria and are best avoided during pregnancy.
3 Vegetables grown in soil that may be contaminated by pets or farm animals can carry a bug which causes a disease called toxo-plasmosis, which damages the foetus. Wash all vegetables (and fruit) really well if you are planning to eat them raw. And avoid handling pets and their litter trays.
4 Salmonella can affect both mother and the foetus. Current advice is still that all eggs must be cooked until both yolk and white are firm. Poultry must be well-cooked for the same reason, as an esti-mated two-thirds of hens on sale today contain salmonella bacte-ria. These bacteria are killed by heat during cooking, so the meat is safe to eat only if has been thoroughly cooked (see also page 29).

> It is a fact that our health does not compare well with that in most other EC countries. The UK – especially Northern Ireland and Scotland – has some of the highest rates of heart disease in the world. The message for individual par-ents is: learn as much as you can, and then eat in the very best way you can, for a healthy pregnancy and to give your baby the best start.

3
BREAST OR BOTTLE

An emotive subject

Until the last century human babies were usually fed human milk. It was, and still is, by far the best food available for a baby. Even the colostrum, (the fluid that a mother's breast first gives when the baby is born), contains valuable nutrients and anti-infection agents. If you can breastfeed for only a few days you will have given your baby an excellent start in life. If you can keep going for a few weeks, then better still.

Bottle feeding is not nearly so good. But formula feeds are the next best thing available: plain cow's milk is not easily digested, being best suited to calves that need to double their weight in a matter of days!

Mothers may find that the choice is not an easy one to make. On the one hand, health workers will be telling them they should breastfeed, and many mothers want to, yet in modern Britain everything seems to conspire against them. There is not nearly enough practical help, and, very importantly, there is a general feeling that breastfeeding in public is 'not the thing.'

It can be quite different in other countries, such as in Norway, for example, where 99 per cent of women breastfeed. There are no advertisements for artificial milks and breastfeeding is regarded as the normal activity it is. To quote one mother:

In Norway a mother can breastfeed her baby anywhere without embarrassment – at work, on the train, in a restaurant, even in Parliament. It is assumed that she will want to breastfeed for as long as possible. It's convenient, and she is surrounded by friends, family and professionals whose experience and advice support her in that choice.

My own experience of breastfeeding in London was very different. It was not done.

Indeed. Some women say they can't breastfeed because they 'can't be at home all the time.' One young mother told us 'I think if I'd had someone to sit with me for the first few weeks, I think I'd have carried on. And my husband didn't like it.' But because mothers are now told (correctly) that 'breast is best', they may suffer enormous pangs of guilt and disappointment when practical and psychological pressures force them to stop. We fully sympathise.

It is difficult in a book like this to deal with all the issues. If you want to read more, start with the excellent book *The Politics of Breastfeeding* by Gabrielle Palmer (Pandora, 1993). We do think, however, the following should be said:

Give breastfeeding a good try. The initial soreness *will* wear off. Get help from a 'breastfeeding counsellor' as early on as possible (ask in your clinic). One mother said

> My counsellor just needed to advise me over the phone! She told me things no one else had, like how to hold the baby right up against me, rather than to lean forward over the baby, to avoid backache and so the baby didn't pull on me. After that I was OK!

If you gave up when you had hoped not to, *don't* blame yourself. Instead, feel free to be angry at the system which let you down and at the manufacturers who worked so hard to undermine breastfeeding. Women have been steadily de-skilled over the decades. As things are now, it's amazing that any persevere.

Most women go on to bottlefeed sooner or later. Whenever you do this, remember your baby will still bond and still thrive. Put your energy now into making feeding times intimate and pleasurable for both of you.

It doesn't have to be all-or-nothing. Some women find it a good compromise to keep the bedtime breastfeed and bottlefeed during the day. You can also change your mind at any stage and re-lactate. Ring La Leche League for details (see page 188).

--------- # The value of breast-milk ---------

For the first few days after giving birth, the first milk that a mother produces is called colostrum. It doesn't look milky — more a yellowish-orange colour — but like milk it's a wonderfully beneficial substance, designed to get all the baby's systems working well. Produced in small quantities, it's a very concentrated food, high in protein, low in fat and rich in antibodies. It is the start that every baby should have; there is no substitute for this amazing food.

It's advisable for a baby to be put to the breast as soon as possible after birth, partly for early nourishment, and partly because it's easier; babies under an hour old are alert and responsive and suck easily.

Breast milk benefits

1   The balance of breast-milk nutrients is incomparable. It also matures as the baby grows to meet changing needs. For the first four to six months nothing else need, nor should, be given: even water is normally unnecessary.
2   Breast milk has a host of immunological and anti-infection properties. Babies breast-fed for at least three months suffer far fewer cases of chest infections, rashes, and other tummy infections like gastro-enteritis.
3   Breast milk protects against childhood eczema, asthma and jaundice. It is thought it may also protect against childhood diabetes, duodenal ulcers and heart disease.
4   Breast milk passes on the mother's antibodies and, during weaning, extra antibodies are produced to help prevent infection at this time.
5   Prolonged, exclusive breastfeeding (at least three months) significantly reduces the incidence of food-allergy.
6   Research shows that breastfed babies become brighter children (about 8 IQ points).

7 Breastfeeding is good for mother too: it helps her body to return to normal more quickly, and it seems to minimise post-natal depression. It's an aid to (but not a guarantee of) contraception.

8 Breast milk is instantly available whenever it's needed: there's no work such as mixing, heating and sterilising to do.

9 It's free! One might also add perhaps that it's ecologically sound: no external energy or machinery is required to produce it, and no packaging or bottles need making and then disposing of.

A few tips

If you can, start preparing to breastfeed early on. You can arrange help: ask your midwife or clinic for a breastfeeding counsellor to be available when you give birth. Start arranging this well before the birth.

Don't worry about preparing or 'hardening' your nipples. Shortly before you give birth, and while you are breastfeeding, your nipples will be regularly bathed in naturally produced lubricating fluid — all you have to do is avoid washing it off!

Give the first feed as soon as possible after birth, if you can within half an hour. After that, aim to keep the baby with you all the time, including overnight, so that she can suckle when she needs to. In this way you both have a good chance of learning quickly how to do it! Sometimes a well-meaning nurse or midwife will remove a new baby at night time ('so the mother can have a good night's sleep') and give the baby a night-time bottle feed. Try not to let this happen to you: it's the frequent suckling by the baby that tells your body to produce a good supply of milk. Any long gaps, such as overnight, tells your body to produce less milk.

Keep your baby at one breast during the whole feed, and offer the other at the next feed. Don't change over in mid feed: the first milk to come is rather watery and thirst quenching, with the richer, calorie and nutrient-dense part coming later. If you switch over during a feed, your baby will get, as it were, two helpings of 'drink' and no helping at all of 'food'.

> Make sure that the baby doesn't have to turn her head to feed, or swallowing may be difficult.

The more you breastfeed your baby the more milk you will produce. The usual reason for failure to produce enough milk is that the baby has been feeding elsewhere. Your body soon gets the message and stops producing milk. You can change matters by letting your baby suckle more frequently, perhaps every couple of hours. If the baby is away from you for a while then express your milk every two or three hours. Give your breasts the message: don't dry up!

If your baby cries, the chances are that he is hungry. If your baby is hungry and wet, his hunger will be distressing him a lot more than his wetness, so feed him before you change him. Some babies get hungry more often than others: there are no universal timetables here! Indeed, old-fashioned feeding schedules and other outdated practices such as separating mothers from their babies after birth or overnight, giving water, bottled milk or dummies at a time when a baby needs to be learning how to get milk from the breast, can all create difficulties.

Aim to breastfeed for a minimum of three months. Even if you don't do it for that long, remember that every day you do, your baby gets an extra day's bonus. If circumstances allow, carry on until your baby is completely weaned. This always used to be the norm, and still is in much of the world. It remains the ideal, and the longer you do it the easier it gets.

It's a very great deal easier when your partner supports you. Let him know how important it is for him to back you up at this time. Perhaps give him this chapter to read. Remind him that a baby with fewer tummy bugs and allergies and so on is going to be a lot less work. Remind him that breastfeeding will help you to get your figure back quicker and, according to some researchers, will make you sweeter tempered! If he says he feels left out, point out that feeding is only one aspect of parenthood, and list all the other things he can do for the baby and for you and any older children. While you recover from the birth and learn to cope with a new baby, it will help if you don't have to worry about household chores piling up as well. As one mother put it 'I didn't need help with sitting down to feed the baby, I just wanted him to get the dinner on!' Fathers have a hugely important role in giving psychological support at this time. Anyway, as soon as weaning starts in just a few months, there'll be plenty of feeding he can do.

Tell him you're going to stick to your guns; after all, babies are more vulnerable than grown men. And then give him a cuddle!

Adopted babies can be breastfed! It may take two weeks or more to get established. Ask your doctor (or La Leche League) for details of how best to do this (see page 188).

Contact TAMBA for advice on how to breastfeed twins and triplets (see page 189).

Formula milks

Women have been led to believe that artificial milks are 'almost as good.' They're clearly not; but they are better than the appalling ones which went before. Be sure to use properly formulated products, made from cow's milk or soya milk and sold as baby formula drinks, not follow-on or baby juice drinks. If you are unsure, check with your health visitor or at your baby clinic.

If you are bottle feeding then make sure you follow the instructions carefully. Over-strength bottle feeds can cause problems for the baby's kidneys. Under-strength can leave the baby hungry again in a short time. If you have any problems understanding the instructions given on the pack, then be sure to seek help, again from a health visitor or at the baby clinic.

Hygiene is also important. The water used for diluting the drink should be sterile. The bottles and teats also harbour germs and must be kept well cleaned and sterilised. And check the use-by or best-before dates on the packs to be sure the products are fresh.

If you have been breastfeeding and want to change to bottle feeding, plan to do it gradually over at least a week so that your breasts have time to adjust and your baby has a chance to get used to the differently shaped teats. Suddenly stopping can lead to painful engorgement and blocked ducts for you, and problems with sucking for your baby.

Don't heat bottles of baby milk in a microwave. The milk is warmed unevenly, so the bottle may feel cool on the outside but may contain dangerously hot milk.

FREE MILK

If you are on a low income you may be entitled to free milk tokens, giving you seven pints of fresh milk or 900 grams of baby milk powder each week. If you are breast feeding then the fresh milk is meant for you, to help give you extra nutrients to boost your breast milk.

4
WEANING

Weaning means the time when a baby gradually moves from an all-milk diet to what are referred to as 'solids' – a rather strange word for the extremely soft textures of weaning foods!

—— Weaning – the first phase ——

When should I start to wean?

Both the UK Department of Health and the World Health Organisation recommend waiting until the baby is at least four months old before starting weaning. They also say that weaning should definitely start before the baby is six months. Breast milk or formula can be continued for at least another six months, and some experts believe that there are many benefits if breastfeeding continues until the baby is two years old. Giving food too early on can lead to the baby developing food allergies and digestive problems. All babies, however, should be eating some solid food by six months as their stores of iron will be running low.

The exact time depends on your own baby. Babies usually find ways of indicating that they are ready to try solid food, and that's the time to start.

When you do start, take it gently and aim to make the whole process of weaning as enjoyable as possible. Don't try to force the pace, either in the choice or amount of food, or the speed of eating. It's not a race! Each baby is different: while one will eagerly eat everything on offer, another will be more cautious. It's the job of the adult to fit in with the needs of the baby, not the other way round. You'll soon be able to interpret all the things your baby is 'telling' you about new flavours and textures she's experiencing!

Anything wrong with jars of baby food?

The purpose of weaning is to make the transition from an all milk diet to a diet eating regular family foods. To wean a baby onto commercial food runs the risk that the food they first learn about may be very different from the food you will want them to enjoy a few months later.

It's very important for children to be introduced to good quality food from the very beginning. It's so easy to drift into the habit of reaching for a jar of baby food, but the contents of these jars and packets are not a complete substitute for real food.

The Food Commission did some research into just what goes (and doesn't go) in to commercially produced baby food and found that:

1 Many ready-to-serve tins and jars are often topped up with extra water, which is thickened with cornflour, starch, various other flours, gums or gelatine to make it seem more like solid food.
2 Desserts and even some savoury items have a lot of sugar or mal-todextrin (a powder starch) which encourages tooth-damaging habits even before the first teeth emerge. Some products say 'no added sugar' but still add fruit syrups, or other types of sugar which still lead the baby to develop sweet tastes and rotten teeth.
3 Since the foods are highly processed and stored for long periods, they have little freshness and the flavours are those of processed foods, just as tinned and powdered foods for adults are not the same as fresh foods. They don't help the baby to get good experiences, but rather give an early introduction to junk. Mothers can be dismayed to find that, after weaning their babies on these foods, the babies go on to reject their mother's own cooking.
4 Nutrients can be lost in processing. Recognising the problem, many companies add a powdered vitamin pill, but there are some doubts that this can properly compensate for the lost benefits of fresh food. Indeed, despite the statements on the commercial

packs which imply that the pack contains all the nutrients a baby needs, the manufacturers themselves admit that they would not advise a parent to rely on their products alone.

5   Foods containing meat do not have to declare how much meat is in them, or which animal species they may contain besides those declared on the label, or which parts of the animal or animals have been used. In fact one 'Turkey Dinner' tested, contained less than five per cent turkey! The average in a 'meat meal' is about only 15 per cent.

Like any processed food, there are some of good quality and some not so good. Look carefully at the ingredients list and see what the main ingredients are, and whether you like the sound of them. If they aren't the sort of ingredients you would want to eat yourself, put the product back on the shelf.

Don't feel intimidated by the very knowledgeable and scientific sounding statements on the packs. If your own meals were analysed for vitamins and minerals and so on they would sound just as impressive, and probably more so! In addition, your food will be fresh and you won't have added bulking agents, starchy fillers and such. Trust your instincts.

Some mothers may think that because chemists' shops sell baby foods this gives the food an air of authority: the setting seems to encourage mothers to think 'If they weren't all right, chemists wouldn't sell them', even though some chemists even sell sweets! Mothers may also be given free samples by health visitors and hospitals, which is an example of how the food industry uses the medical profession to promote its wares.

> We aren't saying you should never use commercial baby foods. They have their place in ease and convenience, and are fine for the occasional meal. But just like processed foods for adults, they should be only a small part of a much wider range of good foods.

Quick-and-easy meals for small babies

You don't have to spend hours and hours making tiny baby meals! A whole month's supply can be made in one morning. Quantities of fruit purées and meat-and-vegetable dinners can be frozen in clean ice-cube trays, and the cubes can then be tipped out into labelled and dated bags, and deep-frozen until needed. If you've no freezer, make a week's supply of meals and store in an ordinary fridge ice-box.

'Meals' for babies at the beginning of weaning consist only of such things as well-mashed ripe banana, or a little chopped, stewed apple, which can be very quickly done on the spur of the moment.

For older babies, simply take a small amount of the food cooked for the rest of the family (before adding any sugar or salt) and mash or puree it as needed.

Don't purée shop-bought ready meals as they are often heavily salted or sugared and may contain all manner of artificial colours, flavours and preservatives that no baby should be exposed to. (If your family has drifted into the habit of relying on such fare, this could be an excellent opportunity to review the whole family's eating patterns!)

Time to begin?

It's probably time to begin solids when your baby:

- seems hungry after a milk feed
- seems to want feeding more often
- after sleeping through the night, starts waking again to be fed
- shows interest in your food
- starts putting objects in her mouth

How to begin

1   Choose a time when you are both relaxed and cosy and comfortable. During or after the midday milk feed often seems to be a good time.
2   At first, offer solid food just once a day, then begin to give solids at breakfast time as well.
3   For the very first taste, try a little sugar-free baby rice in warm baby milk, or a little peeled, ripe, dessert apple or pear, cooked in boiled water (see page 114, and page 117 on how to purée).
4   Offer a minute amount at first, just a taste, and then give your baby time to think about it. You're not thinking of a 'meal' here, only a tiny taste of good things to come!

5 Offer this tiny amount on the tip of your finger. If the new taste is clearly enjoyed then you could offer a little more. If it isn't, wait until another day, and perhaps try a different food.

6 To give more than a mere taste, put the food on the tip of a small, shallow teaspoon (smooth plastic is more mouth-friendly than metal).

7 At first, offer only single foods, one new one at a time, not mixtures, so you can notice any adverse reactions to a food.

8 If your baby shows a dislike of a particular food, withdraw it and try it again in a week.

9 Continue giving a milk feed (breast or formula) at least four times a day. Do not reduce the milk intake.

Don't forget good food hygiene – see page 30.

Then, after about two weeks...

1 Gradually introduce more foods, one at a time, and no more than about three in a week. Try purées of other ripe, peeled, cooked fruits and vegetables: carrots, broccoli, green beans, courgettes, potato, sweet potato, papaya, apricots.

2 Give well-mashed, fully ripe banana (bananas are not ripe until their skins are well-speckled with black).

3 Make a porridge using cornmeal or millet with baby milk or expressed breast milk.

4 At this stage you can begin to combine foods which your baby has previously eaten happily, perhaps potato and carrot, apples or banana and rice. Sometimes puree the mixtures with baby milk. You could mix the milk into a baked, mashed jacket potato.

5 Gradually increase the amount of solids, always, of course, keeping pace with your baby's appetite. Most babies will indicate quite clearly when they've had enough.

6 Continue the milk feeds, and keep the bedtime feed milk only.

This whole first phase of weaning should take about four weeks.

When it comes to teething, forget commercial rusks. Even the so-called 'low sugar' ones can still be very sugary. Instead make your own by baking fingers of bread in a slow oven until hard. Or give toast, or the crust of a loaf. In fact, there's nothing wrong with an old-fashioned bone ring, and you can forget rusks altogether.

WEANING – HOW, WHAT, WHEN?

4-6 months

You can give
Puréed fruit
Puréed vegetables
Thin porridge of cornmeal
  or riceflour
Finely pureed dahl or lentils

How
On a clean finger-tip or plastic
  teaspoon

When
Just a taste at first, during or
  after a milk feed

Not yet
Cow's milk
Citrus fruit, soft summer fruits
Wheat (cereal, bread, pasta
  etc.)
Spices, oats, salt, sugar
Spinach, swede, turnip, beetroot
Eggs
Nuts
Fatty foods

6-8 months

You can add
More puréed vegetables and
  meats such as chicken, fish
  and liver
Wheat-based foods e.g.
  'Ready Brek', 'Weetabix', pasta
Egg yolk (cooked hard)
Small beans (e.g. aduki)
  cooked soft
Ripe banana pieces
Cooked rice
Citrus fruits, summer fruits
Pieces of bread

How
On a teaspoon

When
After a milk feed

Not yet
Cow's milk, except as yogurt,
  cheese or to mix with feeds
'Hot' spices
Egg whites
Nuts
Salt, sugar, fatty foods

9-12 months

You can add
A wide range of foods, offering a
  variety of textures and flavours
Cheese, fromage frais
Fish
Soft cooked beans
Smooth peanut butter
Pieces of well-cooked meat
Well-cooked egg white

How
Use a spoon but also encourage
  finger foods and self-feeding,
  however messy

When
Whenever you wish

Not yet
Cow's milk as a main drink
Whole nuts (until age five years)
Salt, sugar, fatty foods

—— Weaning – the second phase ——

Over the next four weeks:

1 Continue to widen the range of foods, so that mealtimes become interesting and pleasurable events. Try adding purées of lentils, more cooked fruit and vegetables: plums, nectarines, peaches, celery, mangoes, peas.

2 Be prepared to give a hungry baby solids three times a day.

3 Continue to let your baby guide you as to how often you introduce new flavours – and don't be surprised at quite sudden changes in food preferences!

AT THIS STAGE DO NOT GIVE

Any milk, except breast milk or baby formula	Spinach, swede, turnip, beetroot
Citrus fruit	Eggs
Soft summer fruits	Nuts
Wheat (cereals, flour, bread, pasta etc.)	Salt
Spices	Sugar
	Fatty foods

The final phase: six months and onwards

From now on, things get easier! You can gradually introduce more kinds of food, and babies will progress from smooth purées to mashed and chopped food, and then on to whole chunks to suck on and chew. By one year, babies can be finished with 'baby' foods, and be eating what the rest of the family is having, just mashed or chopped up.

Enormous growth and development takes place during these six months, but both often occur in spurts, so the amount of food required will vary accordingly. Your baby will know when she's had enough and when she needs more, so stay sensitive to the way she lets you know when she is still hungry and when she is full.

Be prepared, too, for plenty of mess and wastage. Put newspapers down on the floor, and cover both of you with something easily washed or wiped down and hope for the best! Allow time for your baby to discover what various foods are like: you know, but your baby has yet to learn about it by feeling and smelling as well as tasting and swallowing it. Gradually establish that mealtimes are occasions for sitting down and enjoying good food in a relaxed and sociable way.

It might be easier to think of the six-month transition from early weaning foods to family food as a two-part process, and we will look at the first part (6-8 months) and the second (9-12 months) in a moment. But first a word on milk.

COW'S MILK

There is concern over the safety of cow's milk in the first year, partly because it is low in iron and partly because it can trigger an allergic reaction. The American Academy of Pediatrics says 'not before 12 months' and UK government advisers recommend that cow's milk is used as a main drink 'only after the age of one year' but accept that small amounts of cow's milk may be used to mix with weaning foods for babies aged 6-12 months.

If members of your family suffer from any allergies, then it is recommended you avoid giving your baby cow's milk until at least one year. Otherwise, if you want to introduce cow's milk earlier, try first with milk products like yogurt and cheese and see that there is no adverse reaction. Then mix milk into your cooking. Then, as you baby approaches a year, you can try it as a plain drink.

——— Towards family food ———

Part one: six to eight months

Increase the range of fruits and vegetables. After six months it is considered safe to give citrus fruits, soft summer fruits, well-cooked egg yolk, meat, food containing wheat, and small amounts of cow's milk mixed with other foods.

Introduce purées of meat. Liver and kidney (preferably free-range) are exceptionally nutritious foods, so plan to serve them regularly, perhaps in different ways, so your baby becomes accustomed to the taste. Try it puréed with mashed potato, or cooked apples, tomatoes, leeks or peas: these are all vitamin C-rich foods, and vitamin C helps to release iron into the body.

Regularly serve other iron-rich food such as well-cooked egg yolk, wheatgerm (for example Bemax), apricots, dried fruit, green vegetables, lentils and small beans such as aduki beans. (Remember to add some vitamin C-rich food or drink to the meal, see previous paragraph.) All these foods are high in a range of other valuable nutrients as well, so build your menus around them – and serve them to the whole family!

Try such wheat-based foods as fingers of good quality bread, mashed Weetabix, or a wheatgerm and milk porridge. Use wheatgerm often as it's rich in many nutrients. Sprinkle it over fruit desserts and into casseroles.

For desserts and 'finger food' snacks, serve fingers of ripe, soft-textured raw fruits such as kiwi fruit, banana, avocado and mango. Try segments of satsuma and clementine (de-pipped) and slices of ripe (in season) strawberries to suck and chew on.

AT THIS STAGE DO NOT GIVE

Cow's milk as a drink
Whole pieces of nut (finely ground nut paste, like smooth peanut butter, should be fine – but see the warning on page 34)
Hot spices such as cayenne
Egg white
Salt
Salty processed meats (sausages, ham, bacon, etc.)
Sugar
Fatty foods

Part two: nine to twelve months

Now you're almost there! Just continue gradually adding more and more different kinds of foods. Try to accustom your baby to a wide range of foods early on, so that she doesn't finish up eating only a very limited range of foods and rejecting everything else. It can happen very easily.

- add soft-cooked beans of all kinds
- add pasta of all kinds and colours. Babies enjoy holding pasta shapes and nibbling them!
- try a variety of breads, but avoid any with whole pieces of grain or nuts in at this stage
- give small pieces of well-cooked, succulent meat from a casserole
- well-cooked egg white should now be safe

Begin to give fish; it's another highly nutritious and iron-rich food important in children's diets. Offer individual flakes of white fish at first, but leave oily fish such as tuna, herring, mackerel, trout and salmon until nearer twelve months.

Offer individual flakes of fish either as finger food, or mix it into a little mashed potato or a delicious sauce (look at the recipe section for ideas to tempt all the family).

And we know of one little girl who loved to use cooked, re-frozen fish fingers as teething rusks!

AT THIS STAGE DO NOT GIVE

Whole pieces of nut (finely ground should be safe, but see the warning on page 34)
Sugar
Fatty food
Salt

A few tips

1 Mass produce! Chill cooked foods, then freeze portions in yogurt pots.

2   Make life easier by regularly cooking meals that the whole family enjoys and simply removing the baby's portion(s) before adding any salt or sugar.

3   You can thicken casserole juices and fruity dessert juices with wheatgerm, mashed potato, wholewheat flour or cooked rice (preferably wholegrain brown rice).
     Or you can simply liquidise part of the portion so it forms a thickened sauce. Of course cornflour and arrowroot will thicken food too, but try to go for something more nutritious.

4   You can use plain yogurt, cream or curd cheese, smatana and (plain) fromage frais to thicken food. Yogurt is the best milk product to give first as it is the most easily digested. If yogurt is well tolerated then gradually introduce others.

Drinks

Nothing will quench thirst better than water and there is no need to offer a young baby anything else. If your local water tastes unpleasant you might want to offer bottle water, but taste it yourself first. If it tastes a bit salty or metallic then it may be one of the mineral waters with a lot of minerals – too much for a baby and you shouldn't use it.

Some parents offer diluted fruit juice but this can encourage children to expect all drinks to be sweet ones – and if you set up the expectation now that drinks will taste sweet, be prepared for tears and tantrums later when you try to give anything else.

If you want to offer fruit juices then do so during a meal as then the sugar will do least damage. Dilute the juice so the taste is not too strong (but remember that as far as teeth go, even dilute fruit juices and squashes can be damaging). Don't offer fruit drinks just before a meal or your baby may lose her appetite. And follow the drink with something savoury to take the sugar away from her teeth. (See page 35 on ideas for baby and toddler drinks.) If you can, train children to expect only water or milk between meals to safeguard precious new teeth.

Fresh fruit, where the sugar is well-wrapped up inside the flesh (this is called 'intrinsic' or 'unextracted' sugar) is fine and more nutritious than fruit juice.

You could try a 'savoury cocktail': save your unsalted vegetable cooking water in the fridge, dilute if necessary and offer warm or (not too) cold. Potato cooking water is delicious! The water from carrots and peas tastes quite sweet, but avoid cabbage and broccoli water as it's too strong.

So-called 'herbal teas' and so on sold for babies are just flavoured drinks made largely from sweetened water and should be avoided. Shop around if you want to find sugar-free versions. Buy a pack, take it home and then ask yourself why you are giving this odd powder to your baby (taste it yourself) and whether you are really encouraging the best habits. Then put it in the rubbish bin and notice how you feel. You may well find that making that small sacrifice, wasting the whole pack, will give you a lot of strength for future shopping trips.

Babies' bottles

Use bottles only for giving milk or water. Never try to give either puréed food or sweetened drinks from a bottle. You may have seen quite horrifying scenes in television programmes, showing young children having teeth extracted as a result of being given sweetened drinks very early in life, usually from a bottle or from a dummy dipped in something sweet. Drinks using a straw can also encourage rotten teeth.

Using a bottle, dummy or straw will allow the sugar to wash around the teeth and gums for a long period of time. At worst, this can cause damage inside the gums so new teeth erupt already black with decay.

However, tooth decay is not the only concern. A preference for sweet-tasting drinks may cause other serious health problems such as poor weight gain and growth, lack of appetite, diarrhoea and certain behavioural disorders (see page 34). For a whole variety of reasons, milk and water are the best drinks for your baby.

One other point about babies' bottles: never leave (or let anyone else leave) your baby propped up with a bottle. Apart from the risk of choking and middle ear infection, a baby who is young enough to need a bottle needs to be held, and held warmly and closely. Feeding times can be delightfully intimate and pleasurable occasions for both baby and whoever is feeding her: the two get to know each other! In fact, such times are superb occasions for both social and language development. Make the most of them!

After one year you can dispense with bottles completely. By that time your baby should be learning to use a cup or beaker. Babies who are allowed to have bottles later than that can be very reluctant to give them up. A baby who is being breastfed can continue as long as baby and mother want to. When you start with a beaker, hold your baby closely just as you normally do. Give tiny amounts at first and expect wastage while this new technique is being learned. Make a gradual change from bottle to beaker over a week or two. Avoid letting the bottle or breast drinks spoil your baby's appetite for more nutritious food; it may be best to give such drinks only after a meal.

Tummy bugs

The occasional vomit is to be expected. The odd bout of diarrhoea is common. But if both happen on the same day you may have trouble. And if there is any sign of fever as well, don't hesitate to call your doctor. A baby with a raised temperature should get your doctor's prompt attention.

The common bugs, such as the famous salmonella, usually cause these sorts of symptoms within a few hours of eating something infected. As children love putting things in their mouths they are likely to expose themselves to a range of bacteria every day. But a few bacteria are not a problem, and can even help a child develop resistance. The problem comes when a large number of bacteria arrive in one dose, which can happen with infected food.

The government still recommends that eggs be cooked until the yolks are solid. Don't give babies runny yolks or whites. They also recommend that babies avoid chilled foods which can carry listeria, such as pâté, soft cheeses, cooked meats and chilled ready meals. And there are also problems with unpasteurised 'green top' milk and with soft-whip ice cream (e.g. from ice cream vans and sea-side kiosks).

If your baby is suffering from diarrhoea then offer extra drinks to avoid dehydration.

WATCH OUT FOR:

Unwashed hands, both yours and your baby's, and especially after changing nappies

Pets, pet's litter trays and pet food left out

Raw meat – wash surfaces and equipment after they've touched raw meat

Poor cooking – be safe and over-cook rather than under-cook, especially meat and eggs. And of course, make sure frozen meat has thawed properly before you start cooking.

Poor re-heating – make sure all foods needing re-heating are thoroughly heated up, all the way through, and then served and not left standing around warm

Dirty fridges and cookers, insects and mice

Food beyond its 'use-by' date, and avoid dented cans or any products whose containers are bulging suspiciously.

5

THE TODDLER'S GOOD FEEDING GUIDE

Eating is one of the pleasures of life. If the food is also healthy, there's a double bonus. Food preferences get established amazingly early on, so it's sensible to give high quality fare from the beginning: you are establishing habits now that may last a lifetime.

—— Giving them what they want ——

Although children can't be expected to understand the wide-ranging benefits of good food, they can still enjoy eating it! The trick is to think of all the foods you would ideally like your child to eat (have a look at page 67) – and then devise tempting ways of serving them.

Not all foods are suitable for toddlers so here are a few guidelines:

Milk

Up to a pint a day is considered about right for young children. More may not leave enough room for other nutritious foods.

Use whole (full-cream) milk until your baby is two years old, then switch to semi-skimmed. As a drink, serve it either cold or hot, but not boiled, which ruins the flavour, and not tepid, which may taste unpleasant. Use it also in sauces, custards, quiches and puddings.

Milk products such as plain yogurt and fromage frais, cheese, and smatana make good substitutes for a baby who doesn't like drinking milk, as well as being excellent foods for any baby.

Sugar

All starchy foods get turned into sugar during digestion, so there is never any nutritional reason to add sugar to food. In commercial foods sugar can appear in many guises: glucose, sucrose, dextrose, maltose, honey, syrup, treacle, molasses, muscovado sugar, 'raw' sugar, all of which are worth avoiding as much as possible, mostly because of their disastrous effect on precious tooth enamel. Brown sugar, honey and so-called 'raw' sugar are just as damaging and contain only insignificant amounts of minerals.

Sugar can also lead to a range of other problems such as increased stomach acid, obesity and diabetes. Also, children can become 'high' on large amounts of sugar, with resulting behavioural problems.

Look out for sugar in ready-made savoury foods as well as sweet ones, and also in 'good' or 'health' foods. Fruit yogurts and fromage frais often contain a lot of sugar and not much fruit. (See page 43 on shopping for children.)

Salt

Use little or no salt in cooking. Salt occurs naturally in many foods and there is no nutritional advantage in adding more. Salt can create problems for young children's kidneys, so avoid salted packet snack foods and ready-made meals.

As with sugar, saltiness in food is habit-forming, so keep it to the bare minimum.

Fat

Amid all the discussion about different types of fat, one fact has remained clear: the vast majority of us eat far too much of it. This over-consumption is linked to health problems in later life, particularly to obesity and heart disease. In general, the advice is:

1 Cut down on the overall consumption of fat and oil.
2 Switch to using oils such as olive, rapeseed, sunflower, corn/maize, and soya, instead of solid fat such as lard, hard margarine and butter, although butter can be used in moderation. Cut back on fatty meat and meat products, and go easy on the cakes, pastry, biscuits and fatty spreads like chocolate spreads.

However, children do need some fats: for young children particularly, fat is a useful, concentrated source of energy. Forget 'Lite' and 'low-fat' foods when you shop unless your child is overweight. But watch he doesn't drift into the very fatty sort of diet that has become all too common nowadays.

As your child grows, you'll have to be on your guard: the juiciness and succulence of chips, burgers, sausages and ice-cream is very seductive, but of course that's because of all the fat that's in them!

Dietary fibre

It's also called 'roughage'. It is only in the last few generations that human beings have had much access to refined white flour, rice, pasta and so on. For all the family, choose unrefined, whole grains in preference to their refined white counterparts, as much for the quantities of extra nutrients as for the fibre. However, if you are thinking of changing from white, refined products to wholegrain versions, then do it gradually; a sudden change could lead to unpredictable and excessive bowel movements, a phase which can last for several weeks until the digestive system has adjusted

For the same reason, bran (the fibre found in whole wheat and oats) should not be added to young children's food. Too much pure bran in the diet can stop the absorption of nutrients. Bran, by the way, is not the husk of the grain, as some people think: husks are coarse and inedible and are removed in threshing. Bran is the fine, tissue-paper like layer that coats each grain.

Fruits and vegetables are good sources of fibre. Beans, peas, lentils, sweetcorn, plantains, peaches and strawberries, parsnips and other root vegetables are very good sources. But remember that although these foods are nutritious, they are not calorie-dense, so some children may need snacks between meals (healthy ones, of course!).

If your child needs laxatives, this is a sign that insufficient fibre is being eaten. But laxatives, as well as being (usually) unpleasant to use, can damage the digestive system. Make them unnecessary!

The warning list

Citrus fruits, soft summer fruits, wheat, oats, beetroot, swede, turnip and spinach need to be treated with caution as any of these may trigger an allergy in susceptible children. Give only after six months.

Nuts should not be given to the under-fives, unless finely ground, as with smooth peanut butter or ground almonds. There are particular dangers in inhaling a piece of nut which do not occur with other foods.

PEANUTS

Peanuts must have a special mention, as some people are allergic to them. This type of allergy must to be taken seriously because, although rare, it can be lethal. Symptoms of peanut allergy come up in a matter of minutes, and include a swelling face and breathing difficulties which require urgent hospital treatment.

You may decide you want to know whether your child has peanut allergy. If so, find out in a well-controlled situation. Wait until your baby is well over six months old, choose a time when you know you could get quickly to a hospital casualty department, and then give him a small amount of smooth peanut butter. There will probably be no reaction at all, but you need to know, and it's better than waiting until someone else gives him his first taste – and doesn't recognise the symptoms.

Drinks

Continue to give water or milk (see above). Give fruit juices at meals, diluted at first until they get used to the tastes. Avoid commercial squashes and 'cordials' and any other drinks with added sugar. They contribute little to health. Avoid offering a flavoured, sweetened milkshake at this stage in case it suddenly becomes the only way in which milk is accepted!

Some children drink so many soft drinks that they develop what is now being called 'squash drinking syndrome,' which includes diarrhoea, poor weight gain, lack of appetite and behavioural problems such as irritability. The amount of sugar in some drinks is staggering – a single beaker of blackcurrant squash contains six to nine teaspoons of sugar! Of course, when children consume so much they have no desire to eat. Parents worried by their children's poor growth have sought medical help, but after various investigations, the children improved significantly when the sweetened drinks were withdrawn and replaced by milk and water.

One of the very worrying aspects of all this is that almost all the mothers were perfectly happy with their children's drinking habits! Indeed, it seems that mothers actually conditioned their children to the taste of sweet drinks from a very early age. So now is the time to set up drink habits which don't lead to health problems later on.

TODDLER TEA

Tea as adults drink it is not ideal as a regular drink for children: it prevents iron and other nutrients being absorbed and sweetened tea can be a hazard for teeth.

Still, your toddler can join you in a cup of tea if you:

- make it super-weak: just a teaspoon or two of your tea in a cup of warm water
- add 1-2 tablespoons of milk, and no sugar

And try a mild-flavoured or herb tea such as jasmine.

KIDS' COFFEE

This is a delicious drink for anyone at all, rather like a hot café-crème.

- use all milk, semi-skimmed
- heat the milk quickly or the flavour will change and become unpleasant
- it should be just hot enough to drink, no hotter or again you'll ruin the taste
- add a scant ¼ teaspoon of instant coffee per mug of milk
- no sugar

Additives

Many parents are worried about the added colourings, preservatives, flavourings, emulsifiers, artificial sweeteners, and all the 'E' numbers which are scattered in the ingredients list of processed foods like confetti. And in some ways they are very like confetti, for they are designed to make the food look pretty (or taste attractive, or keep looking attractive for many weeks on the shelf) even though they serve no nutritional purpose at all.

Additives can turn a mixture of sugar and water into a 'fruit drink'. They can turn cooking fat and air into 'ice cream'. They can make cakes a month old look freshly baked, and bacon three months old look freshly cut.

Without additives, the amount of bacteria in a sausage would make it unsaleable in two or three days and the butcher would have to make fresh ones. Without additives the added water in fish fingers would drain out and the coating would look pale grey. Without additives sweets might look a lot less tempting ...

Certain additives are actually banned from baby foods: these include most colourings, some preservatives and the artificial sweeteners. But these additives are not banned from other foods which young children eat, and you can easily find the banned additives in blackcurrant concentrates for 12 month olds, and of course in sweets. Other additives such as flavouring agents are permitted in baby foods even though they have no nutritional value.

SOME CHILDREN REACT BADLY TO

Artificial colours

E102 Tartrazine	128 Red 2G
E104 Quinoline Yellow	133 Brilliant Blue
E110 Sunset Yellow	E151 Black PN
E122 Carmoisine	154 Brown FK
E123 Amaranth	155 Chocolate Brown HT
E124 Ponceau	

Natural colour
E161(b) Annatto

Preservative
E210-219 Benzoates
E220-227 Sulphites

Antioxidants
E320-321 BHA and BHT

The only 'additives' which serve a nutritional purpose are the vitamins and minerals which are put in to fortify foods which might otherwise be very poor nutritionally. A good diet wouldn't need such added vitamin pills, and a poor diet will have problems that extra vitamins cannot address, such as high sugar and fat and too little dietary fibre.

By and large additives do not help children learn about real food. Additives are like cosmetics, disguising and changing the nature of the ingredients, to make them seem more attractive than they otherwise would be.

Worse still, some children are sensitive to additives, and develop allergies, asthma, skin rashes and possibly behavioural problems, when given some of the common colourings and preservatives.

Children with suspected food-related problems including asthma, eczema, skin rashes and hyperactivity should seek medical advice.

Tummy bugs (again)

Remember: diarrhoea, vomiting and/or a fever can mean food poisoning, and a bout of food poisoning can last for several days with a child in bed and in pain. It can get very serious. Call a doctor. And read the section at the end of the previous chapter, on page 29.

6

KEEPING THE PEACE

Imagine a family in which mealtimes are always pleasant sociable occasions, during which everyone is relaxed and conversational, there are no dramas about food and everyone tucks in with gusto and appreciation. Dream on!

No family can be like that all the time. But wouldn't we all like to have mealtimes that were something like that? Certainly those full of bickering and constant battles over food are what no one wants, so it's worth investigating how to make eating as enjoyable as possible; and some research shows that food eaten while one is feeling happy actually yields more nutrients!

Happy mealtimes

Here are some suggestions for happy mealtimes

- do actually have family mealtimes when everyone sits down together!
- serve delicious food
- make it good to look at
- let people help themselves
- talk to each other!
- avoid too much extraneous noise
- avoid fuss and drama

In more detail:

Get together

Try to make sure you all sit down around the table at least once a day. Balancing plates of food on knees whilst watching television is not the same. Early evening and weekend lunch time may be the easiest times, although we've heard of one very busy family who decided to have their main meal of the day at breakfast time, as it was the only time when everyone was around at the same time!

Include your toddler in this as soon as it's feasible. Set his high chair near the table so he can feel part of the family. In addition, plan for you and your child to have a nice, sociable eating time together, just the two of you, at least once every day. It doesn't have to be a 'meal,' just sitting down together to share an orange, segment by segment, will do. But what you'll be doing is teaching him that human beings eat together – and it's nice doing that. Do, incidentally, make a point of *sitting down* to eat: it helps digestion, encourages conversation and there's less risk of choking.

Even quite a young child will pick up the festive atmosphere of larger occasions when relatives and friends come to eat, so do include him in these special occasions.

As your child grows, gradually establish the routine of family mealtimes. Of course no one would expect a toddler to sit quietly at the table until the adults wanted to move, but it's nevertheless worth laying down a few ground rules. For example, when it's tea time, it's tea time for everyone, and no exceptions. Of course it's only sensible and polite to give fair warning, which means you have to be reasonably organised about things! Establish that everyone sits down together for a minimum amount of time. Gulping down a few mouthfuls and rushing back to play is not an option.

Bear in mind, however, that children, especially the very young, don't always get hungry at the five-hour intervals that the adult day is geared to. Your child may get hungry every three or four hours, and so he'll need something to keep him going until the next mealtime. We don't, obviously, mean confectionery! Most of us crave sweet food when we're hungry, but that doesn't mean it is the best thing to have. In this situation there are various possibilities:

Mini-meals

You may need to plan mini-meals of such things as milk, yogurt, a sandwich, fruit, a savoury bun, or soup and toast. Just make sure that the snack doesn't spoil the next meal:

- You might decide to bring the next meal forward a little
- You could serve one part of the next meal now
- You might decide to have a little break yourself, and have something together
- Perhaps the adult day could be adjusted to fit in with the child's needs

Don't, however, put children on a completely different eating schedule. Regularly leaving children to eat on their own, perhaps in front of the television while the adults go to do something else, has been shown to produce all kinds of eating difficulties including food refusal. Eat together as a family as much as possible.

But do feed a child who is genuinely hungry. It's neither kind nor nutritionally right to let a young child's hunger soar, nor does it do anything for good parent-child relations.

Serve only delicious food

Quite simply, if the food isn't delicious, why in the world should anyone eat it? Collect ideas and recipes for high-quality, healthy food that your family will enjoy. Write good ideas down, and perhaps add family comments. Aim for a wide repertoire so there's plenty of variety. Serve favourites often, but also introduce new recipes, new foodstuffs, different cooking methods, so mealtimes become interesting. Avoid the 'We-had-roast-yesterday-so-it's-shepherd's-pie-today-and-rissoles-tomorrow' trap.

It helps to plan ahead: write out weekly menus, and then write the shopping list. Make changes only if you've genuinely had a better idea; not because you got side-tracked/sabotaged in the supermarket (see shopping with children, page 43).

Looking good

This means both the food and the whole table! Whatever your style is for laying the table, it should look an attractive place to eat: clean, organised, and, preferably, colourful. Even a few flowers in a pot can make the world of difference, something that a small child may enjoy helping with.

Of course, the food should look actually inviting. This has a lot to do with colour and colour contrasts, and you can have fun experimenting! Many children are put off by all-white food, so you'll need to enliven it: a sprig of parsley or watercress, a few red berries, pipped black grapes or cherries, a scattering of raisins or of grated, well-scrubbed orange peel, slices of orange, lemon or cucumber. Add pieces of red pepper and carrot to stir-fries and such for their bright colour. Any food with a golden-brown topping looks tempting, so use this knowledge to advantage: scatter grated cheese and a few bread-crumbs over the cooked cauliflower next time and bubble it under a hot grill. Serve it in its dish for everyone to see. Even very young children respond to the appearance of food.

Try a bit of whimsy

- edible flowers (marigolds, pansies, violets, nasturtiums, chives) are fun: scatter marigold petals over milk puddings (English marigolds – French marigolds are not edible), drop chive flowers on the top of the salad, put a nasturtium flower on each piece of cheese
- stand up little 'trees' made of cauliflower or broccoli on a bed of rice or mashed potato to make a mini magic wood. Stand tiny Brussels sprouts in the potato and say baby cabbages are growing
- make faces on little pies or pizzas with halved olives, sardines, mushrooms, salami or vegetable pieces
- arrange items of food on the plate in a pattern
- let your child help with some of these things when he is old enough, so the food becomes 'his'

Sometimes change the setting: perhaps have candles on the table, light them and have a cosy candle-lit meal; even little night-lights in saucers of water look delightful – and last longer than candles. Sometimes have a meal on the floor and call it a 'Rainy Day Picnic' or whatever and serve finger foods, just like a real picnic. Eat outdoors when you can – it's quite amazing how much better food seems to taste out of doors, and also, how much more gets eaten! When you go to feed the ducks in the local park, take food for your own picnic too.

In cold weather, have a fireside tea, perhaps just you and your child: sit on a rug and have hot toast; perhaps you can toast teacakes in front of the fire together. And so on. Make eating fun!

When you bring the food in, behave as though you know it is going to be terrific (whatever happened in the kitchen). If the cook doesn't seem to fancy it, why should anyone else?

Help yourself!

As often as possible, put the food out so everyone can help themselves. By four years old, most children are quite capable of helping themselves very accurately to the amount they can eat – if they're allowed a little practice. Sometimes, of course, they get it wrong, but then so do adults. On occasions when you need to serve the food yourself, give children just a little unless you know they have big appetites. Too much food on the plate can overwhelm children and put them off eating any at all. They can ask always for more.

Talk to each other!

Just that. It's pity to spend each mealtime with eyes fixed on a television screen: the food goes unnoticed and so do the other people round the table. It's frequently a family's only time for being all together. Make the most of it. Try to make sure that everyone gets a turn to talk and no one hogs the limelight. It's an excellent opportunity for language development and social training. Don't let anyone (including adults) turn it into a complaints session!

Make sure you allow enough time for the meal to be a pleasant and relaxed affair, so there's time to talk. No child eats well against the clock.

A bit of peace

You won't be able to have much of a conversation if the television or radio is providing a prominent background noise. Especially with very young children, settle for peace and quiet and keep the atmosphere calm.

No fuss, no drama

If the conversation turns into a gripe, if people are regularly criticised and fussed over because of the amount they're eating, or how they're sitting and speaking, then no one is going to have a good time. Even the food won't seem so good. Of course children need to be taught the correct way to eat things, about asking for and passing things, and, as they get older, waiting for other people to finish. But do it encouragingly and politely. It's counterproductive for a child to feel that every mouthful he takes is being monitored.

Neither should other family members spend the meal criticising the food you have prepared. You know their likes and dislikes, you've presumably done your best and you know it's all good fare. If they don't like it, they may leave it – but there is nothing else until the next meal. Don't get bullied into rushing back to the kitchen to get somebody an alternative and don't allow the grumbler to do it. That's no way to treat the cook! Raiding the fridge afterwards is not an option either. As children get older they can be encouraged to have fun making a contribution to the meal (see chapter 9).

Make sure you've been scrupulously fair in apportioning the food. If one person likes the crispy topping but not the underneath, then he can have his share of the topping: he's made his choice. What he can't have is everyone else's share of the topping as well. Keep mealtimes fair for everybody.

– Keeping the peace when shopping –

Supermarkets know that children will be urging their parents to buy all manner of unsuitable food. It even has a name: pester power. And rather than give parents a hand, supermarkets are only too happy to make pester power work for them. Despite years of campaigning by parents' groups and health workers, many supermarkets still insist on putting sweets at the checkout, where parents and children have to spend time waiting. They rely on you giving in and saying: 'Oh, all right then. Just one. And don't eat it now!'

And there are other tricks. Many shops stack their children's cereals – the sweet ones and often the most expensive ones – at children's height, on the lower shelves. The latest idea being tried in some big stores is to give children their own mini-trolleys, hoping, presumably, that the children will go off to fill up the trolleys with whatever takes their fancy.

It can be a nightmare. All the worst foods seem to have the most attractive labels, with cartoons and bright colours, free gifts and absolutely no regard for healthy diets. What should be a battle between parents and food companies becomes a battle between parent and child. And neither parent nor child will end up feeling good about that.

There's not a lot you can do. But take a deep breath and try some of these tips:

1 Go with a shopping list: it's quicker, often cheaper, and you can truthfully say to a child's demand 'It's not on the list'. You might even have an agreed list which you wrote together before you came out, and which you both agreed to stick to.

2 Have a good meal before you set out. If you shop when either of you is hungry you'll be more likely to get tempted.

3 Have 'good' food ready – take something with you in case hunger strikes before you get past the checkout.

4 Talk to your child about what the people who sell foods do to make people want to buy them. Make it a game in which you two are the clever ones outwitting the salespeople! For example, adopt a conspiratorial tone of voice and say 'Yes, the packet looks fun but let's peep underneath and read what they've put in it.' And then exclaim 'Ugh! It's all toothache stuff! We don't want that, do we?' Or 'There aren't any strawberries in this at all, it's just red colouring. Isn't that mean? And 'They hope people won't bother to read the label, so they'll buy it.' As well as being a good way for you to reject undesirable products, it's also excellent consumer education. If your child thinks he's lucky to have a such a knowledgeable parent – he's right. Not all children get this kind of education.

—— What do you want for dinner? ——

Why do parents ask children this question? It takes a huge leap of imagination even for adults to say accurately what they will feel like eating later on, and even then the day's events could completely change their minds. In any case, you've planned your week's menus, haven't you? So you know exactly what dinner – and every other meal – will be.

Few young children can choose accurately between foods which are not actually in front of them, and asking them to do so leads to confusion.

By all means give older children choices, but keep them simple. Avoid open-ended questions, which could produce the very answers you don't want. Whatever the child's age, avoid questions which invite trouble, such as 'Are you going to eat your dinner today?' or 'Do you think you'll feel like having fish tonight?' If you don't like the answer you get, you'll only have yourself to blame.

Here are a number of tips:

1 Offer a choice between two things only.
2 Make sure they are roughly similar in value, so it doesn't matter which is chosen. For example, say 'orange or banana?' or 'tuna or cheese in your sandwich?' not 'fruit or ice-cream?' !
3 Ask children only about food they are going to have straightaway, not later on, or later they may say 'I don't feel like it now.'
4 If the child cannot make a decision, say 'Then I'll choose,' and after a short while do so. If he then says 'Oh I wanted the other one!' he's too late. Next time he'll know he must choose when asked, or lose his chance. It's teaching him about playing fair, keeping one's word and consideration for others all in one.
5 When shopping for such things as breakfast cereals, never ask children to choose one off the shelf; that's exactly what the manufacturers want you to do! Most children will choose the packet they like the look of, probably one advertised on television, designed to appeal to children: probably expensive for what you get – and probably stuffed with sugar.

Responsibility for choosing the family's food is a serious matter, an adult matter, and it's yours.

———— Visitors bearing gifts ————

It is very kind of friends and relatives to bring presents for your children when they call, and it's important for children to learn from an early age to say thank you and try to look pleased whatever the present is.

The same, of course, goes for parents. But what if the present is yet another packet of sweets when you are trying to limit them?

We think the two following true stories show good solutions:

Julian was a lively, healthy five year old. He had perfect, gleaming white teeth – not something that all five year olds have. He said he liked sweets, and talked as though he had them often, so we asked his mother what her secret was.

She replied that every Sunday after lunch, he was allowed two sweets. That was the only time she allowed them. We asked what happened if someone gave him sweets. She said she would exclaim 'Oh how lovely! You'll enjoy having these on Sunday!' And on Sunday, the sweets would be brought out and two taken. If the donated sweets accumulated too much, then she quietly disposed of some. This, we thought, was clever stuff:

1 She protected her son's teeth by keeping sweets to a minimum without actually banning them.
2 She cleverly gave them only after a meal, when his blood sugar was high and he would be less likely to crave more, and when they had no opportunity to spoil his appetite.
3 Her plan was clear cut and easy to remember.
4 She made the whole deal seem like a treat!
5 She and her son could warmly thank the person who had meant to be so kind. There is no law of good manners which says that children must demonstrate gratitude by eating an edible present immediately they've received it.
6 She stayed in charge. She did not let others sabotage what she wanted for her child.

It's probable that Julian will consume more than two sweets a week as he gets older, but the early years are the most crucial, and usually that's when parents have the most control.

This story is about a two year old:

> Heather and her two-year-old son were visiting the school where she used to teach, and the friendly schoolkeeper gave her son a tube of sweets, a thing he'd never had before. Later, while Heather chatted to former colleagues in the staff room, he played with the tube until it came undone, and then he rolled the sweets about on the carpet. When he grew tired of this Heather gathered them up and took them home to dispose of. One of the teachers remarked on how the boy hadn't attempted to eat the sweets. Heather replied that he'd never had any so he didn't know what they were.

1 Quite correctly, Heather had not felt that the sweets must be unwrapped and sampled just to please the giver.
2 No two year old needs to know about sweets!

If you're challenged about your policy, you could simply say something like 'I don't want him to have to have all the drillings and fillings that I had to have', and leave it at that. You may well find that the other person will immediately agree with you.

A word to grandparents
– and others

There can be a very special rapport between old and young. Grandparents may have more time than busy parents to have rambling conversations with children and often fulfil a useful role in listening to them. Grandparents who do this, and who dispense warm welcomes, hugs, kisses and cosy chats are worth their weight in gold.

We know some who are also giving wonderful support to parents engaged in trying to feed children well, and we know one couple who have provided their grandchildren's only experience of home-cooked family meals. Treats given by grandparents can seem very special, and can be craftily chosen to demonstrate that they don't need to be commercially produced or tooth-rotting: a fine ripe pineapple, peeled and sliced and arranged in a pattern on a plate by grandpa – watched and helped by the younger generation and then eaten by all – might be remembered as an occasional, luscious treat.

Soft fruit or apples from the grandparent's allotment, or some of grandma's home-made biscuits can come to be seen as something rather special – not given away to just anyone! And, of course, presents don't have to be edible. A book, crayons, felt-tipped pens, a comical india rubber, a notebook or sketch pad, knitting needles and wool, a shuttlecock and bat, or something for a hobby are all alternatives.

Why is it that so many people fall into the trap of thinking it is kind to give children presents that instill poor eating patterns, damage health and which lead inexorably to the dentist's drill and worse? Just a little thought could prevent so much.

Part of the answer is that years ago less was known about the hazards of eating too much sugar. Also, British children did not previously get through the colossal quantities they do now: just a few decades ago, sweets and ice-creams *were* treats.

Try not to sour relationships with family and friends over it; if it's only an occasional situation it's probably not worth mentioning. If grandma puts on a wonderful tea complete with trifles and sticky chocolate cake, then eat it with pleasure and appreciation. It's more of a dilemma when someone is always giving your children food you'd prefer them not to have. You could follow Julian's mother's example (see page 46), or, depending on the situation, explain, very tactfully, that your child seems to be getting through so much confectionery now that you think the time has come to cut back. In the end, your children's health is your responsibility.

Changing for the better

If you've decided you'd like to improve your family's way of eating, here are a few tips:

- make no announcements, just begin: If you announce that there are going to be changes to familiar meals your family might feel quite alarmed, and you could have a rebellion on your hands before you've started.
- go slowly, one change at a time. Think in terms of months, not weeks.

Start with changes that are not too obvious:

1 Try different flavours of pasta such as tomato and spinach, then after a while serve some wholemeal, smothered in a delicious sauce.

2 If you customarily provide sweet puddings, include plenty that are based on fruit such as crumbles and pies. Then begin to include a fresh fruit salad from time to time. Try some of the dessert recipes in this book: most are fruity yet quite pudding-y.

3 Begin adding a spoonful of wholewheat flour in cooking, and removing one of white. After a while, change to two spoonfuls, and so on. If you get a complaint, go back one stage.

4 Try different kinds of bread and, very gradually, begin to include wholemeal types.

5 When you serve brown rice, mix dried fruit or vegetables into it and toss with grated nutmeg, cinnamon or paprika. If someone remarks on the colour, you can reply truthfully that you put nutmeg, or whatever, in it.

Make a delicious salad with cooked rice, chopped red and green peppers, spring onions and currants all tossed in a little vinaigrette and bright red paprika. Sprinkle more paprika over the top. Served with cold meats and tomatoes it's an easy and delicious summer meal. Also, try tossing cooked chopped onion, peas and currants into hot rice, and mix in a teaspoon or two of cinnamon and eat it with lamb and roast potatoes – unusual and terrific. (There shouldn't be any complaints!)

6 If you can get everyone to sit down and eat breakfast (and see page 140) they'll be less likely to wilt and crave chocolate bars to boost falling blood-sugar levels.

7 Don't totally remove firm favourites such as chips, sausages or ice-cream. Instead, gradually serve them less often – and be crafty: serve plenty of fruit with the ice-cream; look for a butcher who makes his own sausages; try the oven chips on page 177; serve sausages with a big pot of scrumptious red cabbage cooked with sliced apples and onions; thicken the juice by boiling it up with wholewheat flour mixed with cider vinegar, grated orange rind and a little sugar. And so on.

If you're asked about any of this, say 'Oh I thought it would be a nice change,' or that you think the new ingredient is tastier, crunchier, easier, or whatever; or that fresh fruit is so refreshing in the summer, or you're tired of the smell of frying, or that plain yogurt tastes so fresh and cool, like snow! Have your answers ready so you're not left with something as lame as 'Well, it's better for you.'

Cutting back on confectionery or highly-sugared breakfast cereals is trickier. It might be best to explain to your child what you're doing so it doesn't feel like a punishment.

Choose a moment when you are nice and cosy together, then say something like 'Do you know, I've been reading all about x cereal/sweets/drink, and do you know what I found out? It's nearly all sugar! Isn't that awful? Because sugar can make your teeth go all black and makes them hurt. And if they got very bad, you might have to have them pulled out.' (If reading this makes you cringe, remember it's a possibility and that it will be your child that has to suffer it.) 'Well, I can't bear to think this might happen to *you*, so I don't think we'd better buy x any more, or at least not so often.' Try to think of another less damaging favourite food that could be served more often.

Most children respond when they feel someone has taken the trouble to explain something to them in a friendly and unhurried way, and that a decision comes from serious consideration and love rather than from anger and a whim.

Like-minded parents

In trying to feed your child well, you may sometimes feel that it's just you against the entire food industry. But you're not really alone. Seek out like-minded parents for mutual support. Bring the subject of food into conversation and discover allies. Sometimes having just one other parent telling you you're right is all you need!

If you make allies of the parents of your children's friends, you may be able to agree among yourselves just what you will and will not allow your children to eat at each others' homes. Even if the arrangement falls short of what you would ideally like, it will probably be a lot better than no arrangement at all. You might, for example, all agree on 'no snacks after four o'clock,' so the children have an appetite for their evening meal. Or you could agree to allow a particular food or drink only on certain occasions, or in certain quantities.

One mother we know took her own choice of confectionery – usually a bar of fruit-and-nut chocolate – when her daughter went to stay with a friend. She would say 'I hope you don't mind, but if you were thinking of letting them have any sweets, I would prefer it if they had this. I think it's less harmful than some kinds of sweets.' Whatever the merits of fruit-and-nut chocolate, she made a clear statement about the expected limits of sweet-eating. She said other parents were only too pleased to have the sweet situation settled – and provided!

Several parents have told us how other people's children have enjoyed 'playing at cooking' when they come to visit. Making popcorn is usually a sure-fire winner. Arranging pizza toppings from a range of choices on top of bases made by an adult, making pancakes and filling them, rolling out pastry to make 'snails,' and making 'lettuce roll-ups' with different fillings are all popular activities for older children (see chapter 9, page 73). It's an activity that can continue fruitfully right into the teenage years.

Not all children get a chance to cook at home, indeed, not all have much experience of good home cooking at all. If you offer this type of play, or even just good, filling snacks for children to help assemble, you may find your home is a popular place for children to come to. If you can cope with this, the big bonus is that you will know where your own children are, who their friends are and what they're up to as well as what they're eating. A mother of older children said 'I can stand the mud, I can stand the mess – what I can't stand is not knowing where they are.'

7

BIG EATERS, SMALL EATERS AND FADDY EATERS

We sometimes give children strange labels. We call children with large appetites 'good' eaters, and children with small appetites 'poor' eaters.

What we mean is that children who eat everything that is put in front of them make us, the providers of their food, feel 'good:' they present us with no worry and pay us the wonderful compliment of enjoying our cooking. 'Well done!' we exclaim. 'What a nice clean plate! You enjoyed that, didn't you? You are a good girl!' Whatever difficulties there may be elsewhere, isn't it lovely to find that mealtimes are a success story? We accept the compliment: we obviously know how to feed children! And for the child, how nice to be praised so warmly for something as easy as eating!

How different it all is when our food is rejected. What a waste of our effort! What an insult to our pride! We are affronted, disappointed, hurt. We're also worried: perhaps the child is not taking in enough nutrients and will not grow properly, and if this happens it will be all our fault! Alarm bells ring. And so we try every trick we can think of to make the child 'eat up'. We refute the child's protestations that he's just not hungry. 'You *must* try a *little*,' we urge. 'Getting something into him' becomes a major, continuing project for us. In our anxiety, we may forget our beliefs about healthy eating: surely even a lollipop must be better than nothing.

What a mess! In our anxiety to make a child eat, we use all the worst tricks we know. We may even resort to inducing feelings of:

- guilt: *'After all my hard work!'*
- gratitude: *'Some poor children would gobble it up'*
- pity: *'Just eat a bit for me'*
- defeat: *'You'll sit there till you finish it'*
- shame: *'Your friends wouldn't believe it!'*
  or *'I'll tell daddy / Mrs Favourite-Person at school!'*
- ignorance: *'You haven't even tasted it! It's lovely!'*
- threats and blackmail: *'If you don't eat it, I shan't let you ...'*

Saying such things may relieve your feelings. At least you've tried, and it may even work, occasionally, or at least until the child realises he is being tricked. But it's usually pointless.

What it does do, is turn eating into a contest of wills, which is the last thing you want at mealtime. Also, the more you wheedle, bargain and threaten, the more upset you will become at 'losing'.

——— Coping with rejection ———

1 Leave the food for 15-20 minutes while you eat your own food and chat pleasantly. A child may change his mind while he sits there with nothing else to do!
2 Chat about how clever/kind/sensible the child has been earlier that day. This can remove any tension he may be feeling and spark off an appetite.
3 Praise him gently when he does eat something, no matter how tiny the amount.
4 Eventually, if there is still food left, say something like 'Do you want any more? Are you sure you don't? OK.' And then simply take it away. No fuss, no rebuke, no drama.
5 Sometimes children will eat food they normally reject if they have helped to prepare it. Even helping to lay the table or arranging a few flowers for it can stimulate an interest in the meal.

Remember, no animal or bird worries about their young 'eating up.' We are the only species that makes a problem of uneaten food.

Children may refuse food for many reasons: they may be thirsty (give a little water) or they may feel off-colour or be upset about something. They may just not like the food in question, or think it looks unappetising. Or they may feel under too much pressure to eat, or be trying to get your attention or testing your reaction – or simply not feel hungry!

Whatever the reason, coaxing and anger will not address it; that only sets the scene for future battles. See if there is a problem that needs solving, like an over-full plate (better to serve a small amount and allow for seconds) or something that needs cutting up, but do this in an ordinary conversational way, then let the subject drop.

Even if you manage to bludgeon your child into swallowing something she doesn't want, what about next time? You'll have to decide whether you want to put both of you through the drama all over again – and again and again. And what about the effect of this on your relationship? Even if you 'win', remember there are many perfectly intelligent people who, even in middle age, still refuse to eat a certain food because they were once forced to. They remember vividly the time they were made to eat the detested item, and by whom.

Do remember it's only the food that's being rejected, not you. But if constant refusals are getting under your skin, then put *less effort* into meals for a while. A meal of good bread and cheese with a piece of fruit is fine, and so quick to make you'll feel less hurt if it's shunned (see page 133).

Most battles over food are caused by anxiety, but if your child is healthy-looking and lively, it is unlikely there is any need to worry. If you're concerned about your child's health, consult your doctor (and see page 55).

Why do some children seem to eat so little?

They may be eating more than you think! Anxious parents may be giving soft drinks or squash or cups of milk, biscuits, crisps or chocolate between meals ('so that she's had at least something') but such foods are filling and can actually prevent the child feeling hungry by the next mealtime. If you keep a diary of every single thing that your child eats each day, you may be surprised at the amount.

'Squash drinking syndrome'

A study of younger children by Southampton University found that many of them were suffering from 'squash drinking syndrome', a problem which is described like this:

- poor appetite or reluctance to eat at meal times, with breakfast typically being the best meal eaten
- may have loose stools or 'toddler diarrhoea'
- despite poor appetite, normal levels of activity and energy
- rarely drinks water, often drinks squashes and juice drinks
- may show poor weight gain or failure to thrive

They found that the problems diminished following a cut in the amount of soft drinks being consumed by the child. Soft drinks have become very popular: over half of infant school children no longer drink plain water, while some children are getting a third of their daily energy from flavoured squash.

Cutting back on snacks

The answer to the question 'why does she seem to eat so little' is often that snacks and soft drinks need to be cut back. If you must give something, offer a very minimal item – a piece of fruit, raw vegetable sticks, water to drink or a very small cup of milk, and never close before a meal. You will find this easiest if you simply don't have any of the other types of snacks – biscuits, crisps, etc. – in the house, and then, if asked for them, you can explain in a normal, conversational way that there aren't any.

If a pattern of giving filling snacks between meals has become established, a child may deliberately refuse mealtime food in order to have the snack of her own choice later. She will have learnt that your anxiety makes you glad to give her anything she demands.

Withholding such snacks is again the way to break the circle. Put up with any complaining as calmly as you can for the (probably) very short time until the new regime is accepted.

- of course, if you snack between meals yourself, your child may also expect to. Check your own behaviour
- children's appetites vary in accordance with spurts of growth. Don't expect a 'good' appetite every day
- three and four year olds often eat little compared with the

amounts eaten earlier on. Prepare less food so you don't feel disappointed

- just as children who are destined to grow into tall, big-framed adults tend to have large appetites, children who are going to be smaller need less food. Extra food will make them fatter, not taller!

Feeling unwell for any reason reduces appetite. Constipation is a real appetite-killer. Don't resort to laxatives (see page 33). A constipated child is almost certainly not getting enough dietary fibre (roughage). Gradually swap the refined carbohydrates, (white bread, cakes, pasta, rice, etc.), for more wholegrain versions. Make sure you provide plenty of fruit and vegetables, beans and lentils.

Don't ask for trouble! Questions like 'Are you going to eat your breakfast today?' or 'Shall I give you some green beans?' invite problems. Behave as though of course the food will be eaten. (See also page 44).

Surviving the food battle

Even if you feel very upset that once again your child has summarily rejected your delicious casserole, count to ten and ask yourself if there is some reason behind their behaviour. Sometimes the real issue is not the food at all; it just becomes a vehicle for something else, more to do with the evolving parent-child relationship. Your child may be trying to assert some new independence or test you on some matter – or just feel like playing up.

Food battles can occur simply because the child needs more attention and has learnt that making trouble at mealtimes is a guaranteed way of getting it. Even negative attention can feel better than feeling ignored. Some parents have found that after spending a little extra 'quality' time each day with their children, playing with them, talking and listening to them, mealtime battles virtually disappear.

Remember that testing the grown-ups is all part of growing up, so expect to be tested on food as much as on everything else. It may help to remember, too, that children feel more secure if you *don't* keep giving way. De-charge the atmosphere, remove pressure to eat (see page 53), then change the subject to something more enjoyable.

It is worth noting that children who are 'picky' eaters sometimes have parents who are also picky! Do members of your family spend time criticising the food in front of them? Children are great imitators, so do guard against this. Instead, use their desire to imitate by tucking in well yourselves. Eat with your child whenever you can; don't just watch him while you eat nothing.

Very rarely, a child eats so little over a long period of time that his health begins to suffer. If there is no apparent reason for his refusing food, his doctor can refer him to a special unit at Great Ormond Street Hospital. The hospital usually recommends parents to give the child lots of 'loving, balanced attention,' including 'relaxed family mealtimes with pleasant social interaction between all members'; in other words, happy family mealtimes!

Meals that look and smell delicious

Do make sure your food is really delicious, that it looks attractive on the plate and *smells* good. Check that your menus have variety, and it's not the same old meal over and over. One of the disadvantages of bought meals, of course, is that they *are* exactly the same every single time.

Here is one salutary story we heard:

Eric was staying with his friends, Bob and Judy, and their two small children. Being a keen cook, he offered to cook the evening meal on one occasion when Judy had to be out all day. He also made up a quick chicken casserole for lunch for himself, Bob and the two children, although Bob had some misgivings about the children being given home-cooked food instead of the 'special food for toddlers' that came out of jars! He said Judy was so convinced that such foods were the only sort suitable for young children that she had made a point of never giving them anything else.

Eric had previously noticed that the children ate with no particular relish, and indeed, scattered a good part of their food about them. He was most interested, therefore to see how both children seemed fascinated by his casserole and ate every bit he gave them – and then looked around as if looking for more!

'But,' recounts Eric, 'They didn't seem to know the word "more". They could both talk a little, especially the older one, but it seemed as if asking for more food was something that neither of them had ever wanted to do! Anyway, I gave them an extra helping of chicken and they ate it all, and didn't throw any of it about like they usually did.

'Afterwards, though, Bob made me promise not to tell Judy that they hadn't had their usual jars of food for lunch in case she thought they hadn't been properly fed!'

Take a little time to ensure that your food looks enticing. Children can be put off by food which:

- is piled too high on the plate
- is too mashed or mixed up to be identified
- is hidden by gravy or sauce and cannot be identified
- looks too difficult to cut up or chew
- looks completely strange and unknown
- is colourless.
- looks sloppy or lumpy
- looks like something else they dislike

Take a critical look at the appearance of the food. Just a sprig of parsley, a twist of lemon or orange, or edible flower petals over the fish can transform a plain-looking meal (see also page 106). Even quite young children respond to the appearance of food.

Are you dieting?

If so, don't talk about it! Our modern obsession with thinness is beginning to affect children's health. At first it was just adolescent girls who began to 'diet' as soon as they noticed their bodies filling out, but now much younger children have got the idea that any kind of chubbiness is wrong and 'fat', and some try to 'slim' to 'improve their figures'. It's potentially serious as they can become malnourished.

Counteract this by having family meals of delicious food where adults are seen to eat with pleasure, and where nobody complains about eating too much and getting fat! If you omit sugar, refined carbohydrates and fatty food from your menus you'll be able to eat plenty without worry. Remember, though, children should have some fat in their diets, unlike adults who need almost none.

All in all ...

- eat together
- make sure your food is good, varied and attractively served
- allow children to help themselves whenever possible
- look for obvious solutions like cutting something up smaller, or explaining what the food is
- allow plenty of time for meals
- keep your sense of humour
- after a non-eating child has sat at the table for a while he can be allowed to go back to play, without undue comment

In a normal situation, no child will starve when good food is available. At its simplest, food is fuel: when you have enough for your present needs, consuming more is useless, and will only be stored as fat. Constantly urging children to eat more than they actually need destroys their innate sense of fullness, and leads to future obesity. *Over a period of time* children will take what they need.

Faddiness

Most children go through this stage at some time. In general terms you can deal with it as above.

If your child develops a tremendous liking for a particular food and wants it at every meal, by all means allow him to have it if it's nutritious, but just once each day. At other meals, give him what everyone else is having. If he wants something you regard as undesirable, you don't have to ban it completely but you do have to say it is for certain times only: read 'Visitors bearing gifts' on page 46, and chapter 11 on special occasion food. Beware of banning a food in such a way that you finish up making it more attractive! It may be better to allow it occasionally – and we have heard of one crafty ploy which is to serve a huge portion of the food, and to urge the child to finish it so that he's nearly sick, and goes completely off the idea!

When a child dislikes something, still put it out on serving dishes and allow the family to help themselves as usual. If you're dishing the food up onto individual plates, give the person who dislikes it a very tiny amount without comment. Either it will be left, or, one day, it may be eaten: tastes change for all kinds of reasons. Sometimes, a minute amount of a disliked food served just occasionally along with other food that is liked, can gradually become accepted. Large dollops of it, on the other hand, eaten more or less 'neat' usually intensify the dislike.

They won't eat their vegetables!

Did you, at their age? Did it cause drama at your own childhood meal-times? Do you have unpleasant memories of being forced, either at school or home, to eat bullet peas or over-cooked greens? As a nation, we don't deal with vegetables at all well, and it's really not surprising that children don't like them the way they're usually served.

We're often asked how to 'make children eat their vegetables' so here are a few ideas to try:

1 Don't boil them to death! Over-boiled 'English vegetables' are an international joke. Chop vegetables into very small pieces and boil, steam or stir fry them a few minutes only. Serve immediately. When children reject soggy sprouts and mushy cabbage they should be complimented, not made to eat the stuff.

2 Two or three tiny heaps of different vegetables are less off-putting than a big mound of one kind.

3 Sprinkle them with chopped parsley (fresh not dried) for pretti-ness and a lovely fresh taste.

4 Chop them into different shapes and cook them in different ways. Do you always serve carrots cut into rounds and boiled? Try other ways! 'Carrot chips' are often popular: stir fry thin 'chips' or sticks of carrot in a little oil until just done. They will brown and caramelise and taste candied. Try parsnip chips too.

5 Sometimes serve vegetables as purées. Purée such things as carrots or sprouts with very little potato, a drop of their cooking water and a speck of real butter. (Much enjoyed by adults too – serve these to adult guests and wait to be asked for the recipe!) Look in the back of this book, in the recipe section, for other ideas, but remember you can create your own that your child will like.

6 Children often prefer the taste of raw vegetables, so plan to serve small sticks or chunks or these. Always have some around for nibbles.

7 Bubble-and-squeak is a delicious way of serving greens. Don't wait for leftovers, do it fresh on the day (see page 130).

8 Amalgamate vegetables into composite dishes such as lasagne, soups and stir-fries. Use them as pancake fillings and pizza toppings. Children frequently dislike raw tomatoes, but try a well-flavoured tomato sauce with chicken, fish, or over potatoes and rice (try the recipe on page 156).

9 Encourage children to help with the preparation of vegetables: scrubbing, chopping, and perhaps choosing the shape they'll be cut into that day. Maybe they could be involved with growing some!

No single vegetable is essential. Vegetables of similar colour are roughly interchangeable nutritionally. If your child eats broccoli but no other green vegetable, that's fine. Just have other vegetables available for other family members – and in case of a sudden change of preference.

Don't get hung-up over spinach! Many children dislike its strong flavour and the way it sets their teeth on edge. However, home grown spinach is noticeably less acid, and Swiss chard is also milder and a good alternative. Sometimes spinach is tolerated in a good lasagne, but don't worry if your child never eats it. It's not compulsory!

Offer vegetables as a treat: have raw vegetable sticks as party and picnic food, or bubble-and-squeak as a surprise treat when a friend is visiting. Produce a little plate of mixed vegetable pieces and say 'Let's nibble on these goodies while we watch the next programme', perhaps adding, a little later: 'I love celeriac, don't you? I could eat it non-stop.' And so on. Look at the recipe section for other ideas such as plantain chips.

If all this fails, offer a variety of fruit. This will provide a similar range of nutrients to those found in vegetables. In fact, if you're anxious, look up the nutrients which certain vegetables contain (chiefly vitamins A, C, and E, calcium, iron and fibre) and serve other foods that are rich in these – there are lots. A wide range of good food will cover all types of nutrients.

Never ...

● make an issue of non-vegetable eating. It's counterproductive.
● say 'Eat it up it's good for you.' It makes food sound like medicine! Let them see you tucking in.
● say 'If you eat your vegetables you can have some pudding/a sweet ...' or whatever. This will have precisely the opposite effect and

make the disliked food seem even worse, and if the child doesn't actually dislike the food but is just testing your reaction, she'll soon work out that all she has to do to get a sweet is to wait to be bribed. She may even say 'If I eat all this can I have a sweet?' And whatever can you reply?

Do we teach children to be faddy?

Not such an extraordinary question. It is so easy to pass on one's personal likes and dislikes without realising it. Food writer Roz Denny tells this story:

I listened with astonishment last month while demonstrating a simple stir-fry in a large store. When I offered a small pot of crunchy, colourful, fresh vegetables to a child, the mother turned and said 'You won't like it'. The child obeyed and wouldn't even sniff it.

We encourage children to experience so many things, but sometimes forget to include food!

And big eaters?

This isn't usually regarded as a problem because parents and other carers usually don't worry about it! All they have to do is to make sure they have provided enough food. We would suggest there are perhaps three points worth considering:

1 All food should be nutritious. A child with a large appetite has probably got a lot of growing to do. He therefore needs building blocks in the form of vitamins, minerals and protein to create healthy bones, teeth and muscle. What his body does not need is 'stomach fillers': foods which temporarily satisfy hunger but which fail to provide the nutrients his body is asking for.

The challenge for the parents here is to provide filling meals and snacks that are nutrient-rich, but which avoid refined starches and sugars, and which are not too fatty, otherwise obesity could soon follow.

2 It is easy to feel proud of a child who has a hearty appetite: what a compliment to our cooking! But before rushing to praise him once

again for eating 'so well', remember that all he is doing is satisfying his hunger, which after all, is a rather unremarkable activity. Appetite can vary, and if he becomes less hungry for a period of time and the compliments stop, he may feel subtly pressured into eating more than he wants to regain the reassuring praise. He shouldn't feel he has to eat a lot to stay in favour.

3 If there are other children in the family who eat less than he does, make sure you don't appear to regard his appetite as better than the other children's. It isn't. Similarly, don't call the other children's appetites 'not as good' or 'poor'.

Whether children have large or small appetites, the same approach applies: stay good-humoured and keep comments on individual appetites to the minimum.

8

FOOD AT NURSERY AND PLAYGROUP

The first time many children eat food outside the home regularly is at a playgroup or nursery. Although the food and drink offered may be quite minimal and informal, especially in the case of playgroups, it can have an influence far beyond its quantity. Children may perceive it as food of the big outside world. Indeed, so may parents, as institutions such as nurseries and playgroups inevitably lend a certain authority to whatever they serve.

Good nursery … pity about the food?

If you can find a place for your child where they serve only wholesome, home-prepared fare, with good bread, fresh fruit and so on, you are fortunate indeed. It is more likely that crisps, orangeade, biscuits and chips will rule. It is also quite likely that most parents will accept this without a murmur. Either they will believe such food is quite suitable for children, possibly on the grounds that it's what the children want, or they would prefer something better but don't want to make a fuss. After all, food is only one aspect of care, and if the nursery is good in other ways, and children are happy there, parents may not want to risk being regarded as unappreciative or as troublemakers.

Of course it's sensible to check out the type of food and drink that a nursery is offering when you first go to look round it. If you don't happen to visit the nursery at a meal time, ask what is usually offered. If the answer is a bit vague, you could say 'What did they have yesterday?' or ask if there is a weekly menu you could see. Most nurseries post menus on the parents' notice board. Ask about mid-morning or afternoon snacks in case these turn out to be soft drinks and sweet biscuits! Some nurseries make a special point of serving healthy food, so it's worth shopping around.

One point worth mentioning here: the National Children's Bureau recommends that nurseries should not disrupt eating patterns established at home, so, for example, the nursery should support a breast-feeding mother by giving her baby expressed milk and by allowing the mother access to feed her baby if and when she is able to do so. Similarly, the NCB states that parents should always be consulted about when they wish solids to be introduced and which ones to provide. If you wish to provide your own weaning foods, then the nursery should fit in with you.

However, if your child is already settled in a pre-school group but you have reservations about the food what can you do?

We think it's a good idea to first sound out other parents on the subject. Their opinions may determine whether you want to mention the matter to the staff or not. We're not implying for one moment that you should keep quiet unless other people agree with you, only that you might find it easier to broach the subject if you know you have support. And if you are the only critical voice you need to know it so that you can then decide if you have the courage to proceed!

How exactly you go about approaching the nursery depends on many things, including your existing relationship. Offering suggestions may be taken as making a complaint (which is really what it is). This a tricky business at the best of times, and you have no idea in advance of how your comments will be taken. There may be many reasons why they are serving the food they do, and if no one has ever complained before then the staff may justifiably think that everyone is perfectly happy. Also, if none of the staff has any particular interest in or knowledge of food-and-health issues they may be quite taken aback.

Suggesting changes

There are no hard and fast rules on how to make a successful approach, but we can suggest a few pointers:

1   Do speak directly to the person in charge.

2 Don't write a letter – it's too formal and could seem like an attack.

3 Don't mention it when you're feeling angry! Instead, if the subject doesn't arise in conversation, ask if you could have a quiet word with the nursery head sometime. This will make sure that it will be a good time for both of you.

4 Start by saying how much your child enjoys the nursery and how much you appreciate the good care she is receiving – if this isn't true, why are you keeping her there?

5 Then say that there is one area that you are concerned about. Say, concisely, what exactly that is. Keep it brief. Don't ramble on. If there are several things to mention, make a general statement and give two or three examples. Point out that the type of foods you are unhappy with goes against current healthy eating guidelines.

6 Say exactly what you'd like the nursery to do by way of change, such as to remove its sugary snack foods and substitute snacks without added sugar, for example.

7 Finish by repeating how happy you are with other aspects of their child care.

Whatever reply you get, it will probably be some kind of defence of the nursery's current practice. Don't expect instant agreement or an immediate promise to change everything. You may be told that the food is what the children, or other parents or 'everyone', have always liked. Or you may be told that the cook can't do anything else, or that more healthy food is too expensive. Or you may be told that extraordinary old chestnut: 'You can go too far with healthy eating!'

Whatever happens, avoid getting into an argument about it. You could, however, recommend *The Nursery Food Book*, (see page iii) which is written for nursery workers, and which explains in detail how a nursery can change to a healthy eating regime – and how to balance the books too. Of course any pre-school group can serve good quality food, if it's determined to do so.

After that, you will have to wait and see. If any changes do occur, do be quick to say how delighted you are. If nothing happens, you could try mentioning it again. Of course it helps if there are several parents saying much the same thing. Find out if there are any parent-managers on the management group for the nursery, and have a word with them. Find out if there is a healthy eating policy for your local authority, and whether this includes social services under five's facilities – in which case it should be put into practice in the playgroups and nurseries run by, or approved by, the social service department.

You might also consider getting back-up from elsewhere: contact your health authority health promotion department and community dietitian. They can often offer help such as arranging a talk for parents and working with the staff on healthy eating policies (see page 185).

But keep it friendly. Having a continuing dialogue with the nursery on the subject is fine, but beware of letting it turn into a running battle. Assuming that this is a group which you want your child to continue attending, a happy atmosphere all round is worth preserving.

Good nursery food

We have come across several nurseries that are doing a tremendous job of replacing high-sugar, high-fat and mass-produced foods by home-prepared healthier alternatives. In each case, this 'good food' policy has come about, and has succeeded, almost entirely because of the inspiration of the person in charge: each case is a glowing example of just what can be done with a bit of knowledge and determination. If you're lucky enough to be able to send your child to a nursery which serves good food, do compliment them on it – they will very much appreciate it.

It can also be very satisfying to the cook if she can be involved in making suggestions and ideas, and to feel that she too is making an important contribution to the health of all the children who eat her food!

Good nursery food is based on:

- fruit, vegetables and cereal foods: pasta, rice, and bread of all kinds
- milk, yogurt, cheese, eggs, pulses, poultry and lean meat
- fish should be on the menu at least once a week
- drinks should be milk or water or, if the group can afford it, fresh fruit juice without added sugar
- some fat will be needed in cooking: high-quality, named oils (such as corn, sunflower, rapeseed) are preferable to hard fats

And that's all! The trick is to combine the above ingredients into health-building, tempting meals.

Watch out for:

Refined sugar (such as the sort that comes in packets, whatever its colour), honey, syrups, treacle and so on, should be used in tiny quantities only, and even then not given more than once a day. It's chiefly the frequency of sugar consumption that rots teeth.

Food containing artificial sweeteners should not be used. These new sugar-substitutes may not rot teeth, but they still encourage sweet expectations. As yet they are something of an unknown quantity and should not be regarded as safe for young children.

Salt should be omitted from cooking, and salt cellars should not be put out on the children's tables.

Very fatty food is not suitable for young children. Again, ready-prepared snacks, bakery goods and confectionery are often very high in saturated fat and should not be given out.

Additives may also be something to discuss. If one is not used to it, reading labels on such things as packets of fruit drinks or fruit-flavour yogurts, which are aimed at children, can be quite a shock. You might need to show the nursery just what is (and what isn't) contained in certain items they are serving in order to make your point. It's quite possible that no one on the staff has ever read the labels.

Suitable snacks

Even the smallest playgroup will probably want to give the children something to eat or drink during the session. It can be a very simple affair and doesn't have to entail any cooking. Fingers of good bread, cubes of cheese and little scrubbed vegetable sticks, pieces of fresh or dried fruit can be put out in various combinations.

It's interesting, and educational, for children to have different types of bread to try: French sticks, rye, wholewheat, nan, chappatis, flat Greek loaves – whatever can be bought in the local area.

Most vegetables can be eaten raw: carrots, parsnips, celeriac, celery, courgettes, red peppers (they're sweeter than green), cauliflower and fresh peas. And almost any kind of fruit could be offered, perhaps cut up immediately before being eaten. Raisins, sultanas, and pieces of dried apple, pear and apricot are popular with children. Dates are less suitable in that they are both exceptionally sweet and also very sticky.

If the pieces of food are cut up in a variety of different shapes – circles, sticks, long diagonals, cubes, chunks, triangles – they can seem more attractive and 'different' to children. They can be served separately, or together as a salad, or with a yogurt-based dip.

So there's plenty of scope! No need at all for sugary or salty packet snacks, so high in price and so poor in value.

If it's the custom for parents to send food for their children to eat mid-morning, the nursery or playgroup needs to have some kind of policy on this. The easiest one is 'fresh fruit only': it's clear what it means, it's healthy, and it keeps out sticky or greasy food. If each child brings her fruit in a bag with her name on it and puts it into a designated container, it's easy for the staff to give the fruit out later.

Nursery dinner

If a nursery provides a mid-day meal, there are all kinds of delicious, nutritious dishes it can serve without resorting to a routine of chips, burgers and sausages. One nursery we found serves a wonderful array of main course dishes, including home-made lasagne and pizzas, chicken and vegetable pie, Nasi Goreng, lentil moussaka, marinated chicken drumsticks with fried rice, coconut curry, vegetarian pasties, fish rissoles, jacket potatoes with cheese and ham, vegetable pasta and chicken in peanut sauce.

Each day there is a choice of at least two salads in addition to any cooked vegetable that may be served. Bread is always available.

Desserts are built around fruit. The most usual dessert is simply pieces of fresh fruit to eat as finger food, although sometimes fruit is stirred into plain yogurt with a little fresh orange juice, or there's a mixture of fruits in a salad. Occasionally, the fruit is served cooked in a crumble or pie, or there's a virtually sugar-free carrot cake or banana bread. Or there may be cheese and fruit or cheese and crackers. All very simple to prepare.

This particular nursery asks parents to donate fruit on a regular but informal basis. Each day, the staff collect up the donated fruit, sort it, and prepare it for use in a mid-morning or tea-time snack. This helps the nursery with its budget, and parents are actively involved in helping to promote healthy eating.

Incidentally, nurseries are supposed to provide a certain multicultural aspect, i.e. dishes representing a variety of countries rather than just one. The above list of main-course dishes is a good example of this; it also provides very interesting eating.

Food activities

Why is it that so many people (even childcare professionals) think that children's cooking means making cakes? And not only that, but cakes covered with icing, sweets and all manner of tooth-rotting goodies! Of course it's nice to bake cakes once in a while, but this shouldn't be a child's only experience of cooking. In fact, as most children are keen to consume what they have made – for one thing they know exactly what's in it – this presents wonderful learning opportunities on the subject of healthy food.

Parents sometimes help with cooking activities, so if you're involved in this, you might consider suggesting that you made something savoury: cheese scones, cheese straws, pizzas, or perhaps bread rolls, or even a vegetable soup. Don't criticise cake-making when you go, just enthuse about the taste of what you've all made. (Look for ideas in chapter 9.)

Birthdays at nursery or playgroup

This is when good practice can sometimes fly straight out of the window. It has to be said that some parents are partly to blame here: it is not unusual for a mother to come armed with an enormous shop-bought cake or with an array of sweets, biscuits, chocolate bars and even fizzy drinks so that the nursery can give her child a party. Whatever the feelings of the nursery staff, there is little that can be done at this stage. It is difficult for a nursery to refuse food which has already been bought and when the birthday child is excited about her party.

Of course birthdays are hugely special to children, and of course nurseries and parents both should do something by way of celebration, but there are ways of doing this that don't risk either the children's teeth or getting grease and food-dyes on books, toys and clothes. It may be 'only once a year' for an individual family, but for a nursery it could happen several times a week.

Some nurseries (and infant schools) have a special ceremony at which the birthday child lights the candles, with a long taper, on a pretend birthday cake (easily made from a plasticine-filled tin, covered with pretty paper with big candles stuck in). Other ideas are for the child to be able to sit on a special cushion or chair, or to wear a 'birthday hat' or sticker. And, at some stage, of course, the birthday song will be sung.

Some parents do like to bring in an edible treat, however, and one excellent way of dealing with this is for the nursery to say (again) 'fresh fruit only'. A few satsumas or rosy apples can be easily divided up at a little 'party'. Other ideas are seedless grapes, a ripe pineapple or a few pears, a pink melon, big golden gooseberries, strawberries or peaches. If they want to, the staff can make much educational use of the fruit, such as the mathematical puzzle of dividing it up fairly.

But you don't have to wait until your child's nursery decides to adopt this policy. If other parents take their choice of treat, then you can take yours. But do mention it to the staff beforehand: they may be surprised! If you don't know how your suggestion will be received, offer something difficult to refuse like strawberries.

One extra benefit of a 'birthday fruit' policy is that the competitive element over size and grandeur of birthday cakes is removed, along with much of the expense, which can be a relief all round.

All in all, don't wait for you local children's group to discover healthy foods: give them a little (diplomatic) help!

Childminders

Establish whether you or the childminder will provide food, and discuss exactly what you both mean by 'providing food'. Of course, any childminder should aim to fit in with what you want for your child, and try to make eating a pleasant affair. If, for example, you request that your child has milk to drink and not juice, the childminder should respect that. Make sure that it's clear who is expected to buy it. If the minder has other children besides yours, find out how your child will fit into her eating arrangements.

If you're providing the food, look at the ideas for snacks and meals in the recipe section. In winter, a flask of hot soup could be good, too. A simple meal or snack of good bread, cheese and fruit with a glass of milk is excellent for any time and has endless variations (see page 133). For babies, you could send your own frozen mini-meals to be thawed and re-heated at the last moment. Note the story of one mother who told us:

'My baby always had bought food because I wanted to make it easier for the childminder, but later she wouldn't eat my food! I had to do a sort of second weaning onto my cooking.'

9

COOKING WITH YOUR CHILD

'Playing cooking' is good fun, especially if there's something good to eat at the end of the game. This chapter has some ideas for different types of cooking that children can do at home. You'll be able to add other ideas that suit your own family.

Young children will think of cooking as a form of play (they don't distinguish work from play anyway) so leave plenty of scope for creativity and imagination. In fact, like other forms of play, cooking is educational: through cooking, your child will become familiar with counting, size, shape, fractions, weighing, time, capacity, volume, absorption, heat, freezing, thawing, dissolving ... all basic mathematical and scientific concepts which adults take for granted but which children have to learn. It can be 'learning through play' at it's best.

By four years of age, most children will be able to enjoy an easy cooking activity. But before doing any cooking you may want to make pretend foods out of playdough, which can take any amount of ill-treatment, and no one is going to eat it, (there is a recipe for playdough on page 77). When your child can manipulate it reasonably well try real dough – see pastry ideas on page 78. Other mixtures made with the fingers can also be tried: with supervision, children of this age can help knead small amounts of bread dough, wash and dry salad greens, chop and stir fruit into yogurt and even chop vegetables for soups or stews. The more they do it the more adept they become!

Preparing to cook with your ____ children's help!

First check that you have everything ready. A child will get bored waiting while you hunt for something at the back of a cupboard or decide which carrot to use. So before you start:

1 Check all the ingredients are out.
2 Check all the cooking utensils are out, clean and ready to use.
3 Think if you need to do any preparation beforehand – and have it done.
4 Use newspapers or plastic sheeting to cover the cookery area, and aprons to cover all the cooks. You'll be less anxious when things get spilled if you know everything's well protected.
5 Find a work surface that's the right height for a child. Improvise if necessary. It's not a good idea for a child to stand on something to make him higher: sooner or later he's bound to tip off. At a pinch, work on the floor on a large plastic sheet.
6 Make a safety check – have you left a sharp knife out, a burner on or a spillage not mopped up? Make sure the kitchen is *safe* for a child, even though he'll be supervised the whole time.
7 Allow lots of time in case it takes longer than you'd guessed.
8 Remember the activity is chiefly for the child's benefit. His enjoyment and satisfaction is more important than the end result. (How good were your first efforts at cooking?)
9 Make it fun, so he wants to do it again.

Sometimes, when you're cooking normally, ask your child if he would like to help: perhaps he could make the decorations for the top of the pie, or chop up the carrots for the casserole, or help stir the pudding and so on. And don't forget the wonderful job of scraping the bowl out!

As children get older they should be gradually taking on their share of family responsibilities, and if this includes cooking, they will acquire important lifetime skills. One recent survey found that children were more likely to know how to programme a video recorder than how to boil an egg! It is in nobody's interests to have a child or teenager who is helpless in the kitchen, and a hungry child who can make himself a tasty snack may be saved from automatically going to buy a chocolate bar. Looking further ahead, your child may one day have to feed himself away from home on limited means, and he'll have a far better chance of staying fit and well if he has a few cooking skills.

WHY TEACH YOUR CHILDREN TO COOK?

- because it's unlikely anyone else will
- because it's fun
- because it's a satisfying activity for a parent and (especially) a young child to do together
- because it's creative
- because it's educational
- because it's tactile
- because it encourages self-sufficiency
- because one day it could stop your children living off packets and tins and TV dinners. They'll be fitter and richer.

———— Kitchen pleasure ————

Try to remember at all times that the aim is to have fun. There are always plenty of jobs to do in the kitchen, but as children get older, avoid using them as unpaid scullery maids, doing the jobs that you don't want to do. That could put them off for life. Find a part of a meal or recipe that's complete in itself, so the child's contribution is obvious. Just letting children have a stir of something won't make them think they've 'made' it. Older children might produce an entire dish, but below are a few ideas for young children.

1 Washing salad greens. A lovely messy outdoor activity for warm weather. Have a little water in a large bowl and use plastic aprons – or swimming gear! When the greens are washed they can be shaken dry and then whirled (by you) in a tea-towel to finish.
2 As above, but scrub potatoes, carrots, beetroot and other such vegetables. Put the scrubbed vegetables into a colander and rinse under the tap.
3 Manually adept children are quite capable of chopping vegetables for soups and casseroles. You don't have to ban sharp knives, but

you do have to be sure they know what dangers there are, that they have to be 'grown up' about using them, and how to hold them. The knife must be fairly sharp or it won't cut and then the child will have to press too hard, which *is* dangerous. Of course you will stay close by all the time. If it sounds too alarming, don't do it, although it's not an uncommon activity in nursery schools. Make sure the surface they cut onto isn't slippery – always put a damp cloth on the table under the chopping board, so it won't slide about. It's a good tip for any cook: a damp cloth under a mixing bowl or chopping board grips it and holds it still.

4   Blanching almonds: Place the almonds in a small saucepan, bring to simmering point in plenty of water, turn off the heat and leave to soak for about 15 minutes. Remove one, nip off the brown skin at one end, and see if you can squirt it out of its skin. If you can't, leave them all to soak a bit longer, perhaps re-heating their water. When the almonds are ready, ask your child to help you squirt them out of their skins – but choose where you do it. Aim them downwards into a large bowl, but be prepared for a few escapes.

5   Shelling peas. Show how to pop them open and to check for maggots, and then the child can carry on. If some get eaten so much the better. Some people prefer peas raw.

6   Shelling broad beans. How differently to peas the beans are packed in their pods! Worth doing at least once for the contrast.

Your own way of cooking will suggest more ideas. You can gradually increase your child's skills repertoire to include using lemon squeezers, graters, and so on. And you never know where it will end; you may have a future chef in the family!

CLEARING AWAY AND WASHING UP

It's all part of the job. Make it a rule that everyone who has cooked helps to clear up – well, you can try, anyway. Even young children can help by carrying utensils to the sink or putting something away.

Playing with recipes

PLAYDOUGH

Make up this basic recipe with your child. It could also be fun to make this with two or three children. When they can handle it well, you could go on to edible pastry, as below.

1 mug plain flour
1 mug salt
a teaspoon or so of oil
water to mix, about half a cup

Use as an all-purpose modelling material. Make sure children have plenty of time for free play with it. Avoid trying to get them to make something you would like them to make or 'showing them how': adult art and child art are two very different things. Children need to find out how to do things, not to copy anyone else's version. If you keep showing them your adult way you'll spoil their fun and make them lose confidence in their own ability.

If they ask you what they can make, suggest general ideas. You could suggest some pretend food for 'playing house', which could be baked in the oven so it will keep. Or you could suggest making a model of themselves, or of a pet, a funny face, a snake, a cartoon character, a model of something in their home – or 'something that will surprise me!' Then let them do it their own way. Be appreciative of the result and let them tell you about it.

Playdough models can be baked for up to two hours in a moderate oven. After cooling, they can be painted and varnished. Otherwise, keep the dough moist for another day by storing in the fridge in a tightly sealed container.

Pastry ideas

Let children have fun working with real pastry: mixing, rolling, shaping, but don't let it all go on too long as it is eventually supposed to be eaten. You can say that playdough is for playing with, but this is food and it will spoil if it's handled too much. Hard margarine would do instead of butter and might be a good idea at first if you think there'll be a lot of wastage. Soft margarine won't work at all.

PASTRY-MAKING

Children love fiddly activities, so find recipes which provide lots for small fingers to do. Pastry-making is ideal in this respect, and has the added excitement of being baked. It's also versatile: it can be used in all kinds of savoury and sweet dishes, and has many variations such as the little cheese biscuits below. Just make a small quantity each time, and remember you don't have to eat it all!

Cooks take note! The recipe here is exceptionally delicious; use it yourself for quiches, mince pies and so on. The higher fat content makes it easy to handle and prevents it cracking easily. It therefore can, and should, be rolled out very thinly, so, mouthful by mouthful, less fat is eaten than with other kinds.

BASIC PASTRY

75 g (3 oz) plain flour*
50g (2oz) butter
tiny pinch of salt
3 teaspoons of very cold water

* (White is easier to handle, so sieve some with a just little wholemeal at first. Increase the wholemeal as expertise develops.)

1 Weigh the ingredients with your child – use balance scales if you can as they are ideal for educational weighing.
2 Put the flour, salt and butter into a big bowl on a surface that your child can reach into easily.
3 Take it in turns to cut the butter up into the flour using two blunt knives until it's in very tiny pieces.
4 Rub the butter in with your fingertips until it all looks like coarse breadcrumbs. You could do this together. For the best pastry, rubbing in should be done lightly and quickly, using only the fingertips, but with a very young beginner, the process could go on a bit longer if it's being enjoyed.

5 Drop in the 3 teaspoons of cold water, counting as you go. Either
   do this yourself, or let your child measure them out – into a separate bowl first in case of mistakes.

6 Cut the water in with a knife and then press and squeeze with the
   hands to make a dough. By now, the dough has probably got warm
   and sticky, so pop it in a covered bowl in the fridge for about 20
   minutes to make it easier to roll out.

7 Take it out and re-knead it into a few small smooth, crack-free
   patty-shapes.

8 Roll out the shapes one by one on a lightly floured smooth table
   top or other surface. Don't use a wooden board unless you have an
   enormous one – it just makes things more complicated. Flour a
   rolling pin and do the first couple of rolls yourself, then let the
   child carry on. If you have a child's-size rolling pin so much the
   better. Keep lightly re-flouring the work surface and move the
   pastry about after every few rolls. Keep re-flouring the pin too, or
   the pastry will stick to it.

9 When the pastry is thin enough, proceed with the recipe you've
   chosen. If the pastry is stuck, push a palette knife or fish slice
   underneath to lift it up. If it comes to bits, simply patch it up –
   patches will seal during cooking.

Clean sticky dough off your hands by rubbing flour on them, then
they'll be easier to wash.

PASTRY SNAILS

1 Using a blunt knife, cut small strips of pastry, about one inch
   (2 cm) wide and 2-3 times as long.

2 Sprinkle/spread the pastry lightly with grated cheese or yeast
   extract or a little sugar and cinnamon mixed together. Roll up.

3 Place the rolls on a lightly greased baking sheet on their curved
   side (otherwise the filling with fall out too easily), with the fold
   underneath to keep the snails rolled up.

4 Bake for about ten minutes, depending on the thickness of the
   dough, at a high temperature, gas 6-7, 400-425°F, 200-210°C. Eat
   hot or cold.

CHEESE BISCUITS

Make the pastry as above, but add:

● a pinch of cayenne pepper or mustard

- a pinch of black pepper
- about an ounce of grated cheese
- 2-3 drops Worcester sauce

Roll out, not too thinly this time, and cut into a variety of shapes, perhaps using a pastry cutter.

Bake on a lightly oiled baking sheet at gas 6, 400°F, 200°C for about 10 minutes.

SESAME CHEESE BISCUITS

As above, but press sesame seeds into the pastry just before the final rolling.

PASTRY PIZZAS

This is a 'play' version of the tomato pie recipe on page 157. You will need:

plain pastry made as above
a small quantity of tomato sauce (see page 156)
a little grated cheese
various pizza toppings, such as mushrooms, olives, ham, salami, tuna,
  sardines, parsley, oregano, etc.

any kind of small, shallow tartlet tins

1 Roll out the pastry, cut out circles and line the tartlet tins. With a fork, prick each circle in two or three places right through, so they don't balloon upwards during baking.

2 Bake for about 10 minutes at gas 6, 400°F, 200°C. Leave in the tins and allow to cool a little. Put a flat teaspoonful of tomato sauce into each circle of cooked pastry.

3 Sprinkle with grated cheese and decorate with pieces of topping.

4 Put back in the oven for a minute or two to heat through just before eating.

   Variation: instead of tomato sauce, just have a slice or two of fresh tomato.

CHEESE SABLÉS

These delicious sablés make an excellent pre-dinner appetiser for both adults and children.

50 g (2 oz) butter
50 g (2 oz) grated cheese
50 g (2 oz) plain flour
tiny pinch salt and pepper

1   Cut the butter into the flour with two knives, as in the main pastry recipe, then rub in with the fingers. Chill in the fridge for a few minutes.
2   Roll out thickly: almost 1 cm (¼ inch), and cut into shapes. Sablés should really be triangular, but other shapes will taste just as good!
3   Bake on greaseproof paper on a baking sheet for 10 minutes at gas 5-6, 375-400°F, 190-200°C.

PHILIPPA'S BLUE CHEESE BALLS

Philippa is a professional nursery school cook. She devises all kinds of delicious recipes. This recipe will make 30-35 tasty nibbles.

1 cup wholemeal self-raising flour (or just sift half a teaspoon of
*   baking powder into a cup of plain wholemeal flour)*
1 cup rolled oats (not jumbo)
1 ¹/₂ cups grated blue, or any, cheese
3 tablespoons of melted butter
half a cup of milk
1 egg

1   Combine the flour, oats and cheese. Stir in the butter.
2   Beat the egg, stir it into the milk, and stir into the other ingredients.
3   Using the fingers, shape teaspoonfuls of the mixture into little balls and place on a lightly oiled baking sheet.
4   Bake at gas 6, 400°F, 200°C for 15 minutes.

LETTUCE ROLL-UPS

Fill lettuce leaves with any of the following and roll up! Fold the 'sides' of each lettuce leaf in as you roll to keep the parcels neat and to enclose the filling securely.

Keep rolled by placing them close together in a serving dish. Use the leaves of an ordinary 'round' lettuce.

- grated carrot and sultanas
- cottage cheese and pineapple
- tuna and cucumber
- apple and celery
- smooth peanut butter
- chopped ham and curd cheese.

KIDS' COLESLAW

Children who are old enough to slice raw fruit and vegetables can make their own 'personal' coleslaw; and choosing the ingredients may make them keen to eat it! Slice the cabbage (finely) for younger children.

Carrot, apple, red or white cabbage and celery can be grated or sliced; and seedless grapes, raisins, sultanas or chopped dried apricots added for sweetness.

Toss in a little mayonnaise, possibly mixed with smatana, yogurt or cream. For fun, make 'pink mayonnaise' by stirring in a dash or tomato puree or ketchup, or turn it yellow with a pinch of turmeric. Some cooked, shredded beetroot will turn it another colour! Have fun experimenting.

CRUNCHY BANANAS

A quick nursery dessert that tastes sweet without any sugar.

bananas
a little fresh orange juice
a little desiccated coconut or good muesli

Cut each banana into chunks, roll in orange juice, and then in desiccated coconut or a good muesli (without nuts).

PHILIPPA'S RAISIN AND CARROT LOAF

Another good, sweet dish made without sugar.

1 egg
¹/₄ cup of milk

200g (8 oz) cottage or curd cheese
generous ¹/₂ cup grated carrot
³/₄ cup raisins
1 level teaspoon mixed spice
2 cups self-raising wholemeal flour (OR sift 2 rounded teaspoons
  of baking powder into wholemeal plain flour)

1 Lightly beat the egg with a fork in a bowl. Mix in the milk.
2 Stir in the cheese, carrot, raisins and spice.
3 Stir in the flour and make a dough. Press into a lightly oiled small
   (1 lb) loaf tin.
4 Bake at gas 6, 400°F, 200°C for 30-40 minutes.
5 Cool on a wire rack – or across the bread tin.

SWEDISH OAT BISCUITS

If you want to make some individual cakes, this recipe is delicious
while being healthier than most cake recipes. The original recipe had
much more butter and sugar in and yet our version doesn't taste
noticeably different. It's a good example of how you can change many
conventional cake recipes to make them healthier.

75 g (3 oz) plain wholemeal flour
75 g (3 oz) rolled oats (not jumbo)
100 g (4 oz) butter or sunflower margarine
25-50 g (1-2 oz) sugar

1 Have the butter ready melted.
2 Mix the flour, oats and sugar into a bowl. Stir in the melted butter.
3 With the fingers, roll and shape the mixture into 12 little balls,
   each about the size of a walnut.
4 Place these on a lightly greased baking sheet and flatten lightly
   with a fork.
5 Bake at gas 5, 375°F, 190°C for 12-15 minutes, or until a light
   golden brown. Eat warm or cold.

HOME-MADE FRUIT YOGURT

You may be surprised to discover how easily – and cheaply – you can
make yogurt at home, using only a vacuum flask. Use a wide-mouth
flask so you can get the yogurt out easily.

Basic yogurt mixture:

1 small carton Long-Life (UHT) milk
1 teaspoon ordinary plain yogurt
2-3 tablespoons powdered milk

1   Mix a little of the milk with the teaspoon of yogurt in your flask.
2   Heat the remaining milk in a saucepan to rather hot but nowhere near boiling. 115°F is about right, but you can test the temperature with your finger. If the milk is right it should feel distinctly hot, but not so hot that you can't bear to leave your finger in the milk for a second or two. There's quite a bit of leeway, so don't be too anxious about exact temperature.
3   Whisk the milk powder into the hot milk, then tip it all into the flask and stir.
4   Seal the flask tightly and leave undisturbed – a high shelf is a good place for it – for at least six hours.

At the end of that time, remove the lid and, hey presto! You have a flask of set (and warm) yogurt. This is a moment of amazement bordering on magic to children – and some adults. Explain how the yogurt has grown in the warmth of the heated milk and turned all the milk into yogurt. You could also explain that it's the *acidophilus* bugs in the yogurt that did the work: children love long names.

Chill the yogurt in another container until you want to eat it.

IF THE YOGURT DIDN'T SET
If the yogurt didn't set, and you know the flask wasn't moved while it was setting, then the milk was either too hot or too cold. Simply try again using the same milk and a fresh teaspoon of yogurt.

FRUIT YOGURT

It's really worth making your own fruit yogurt, even if you use bought plain yogurt instead of home-made. Shop ones are heavily sugared and contain little or no real fruit.

plain yogurt
a little fresh orange juice
any fruit(s) of your choice

1 First stir a little orange juice into the yogurt to sweeten it. No other sweetening is needed.
2 Mash some of the fruit and mix it evenly into the yogurt. Chop the rest and stir in.

Children often say they don't like the 'bits' (of fruit) in bought yogurt; hardly surprising, since these are usually unrecognisable and have the texture of sawdust. The 'bits' in yours will be different: whole slices of strawberry, raspberry, satsuma, cherry, banana or nectarine. If your child likes smooth fruit yogurt you can blend it. Try mashing blackberries into yoghurt and see the brilliant purple colour. (You may need to add a pinch of sugar to this one. A small pinch of mixed spice cuts the sharpness well, too.)

Young children can easily mash and chop ripe fruit and stir it into yogurt, and enjoy stirring the two colours together to make a new one.

FISH

It's really true that some children believe that fish have fingers. Too bad that fish fingers seem to be their only experience of fish, which can be so delicious when properly prepared. Amazing, too, that some children are so unfamiliar with what fish look like.

Make sure your child knows better. Buy a whole fish from time to time and look at it together. Explain what the fins do and feel the slipperiness of the unwashed fish, while you say how fish need to be slippery to swim easily through the water. Show the tiny sharp teeth – fish need to bite their food too!

Older children might be interested in the preparation of the fish, but in any case do show the fish bone – in a way a bit like ours: a spine with ribs growing out of it! (See the recipe for Scottish Herring, page 142 for an easy way of getting the bone out.)

Most fish have a rather dry taste, so make sure you serve fish with moist and tasty accompaniments. Never overcook fish or it will taste appalling. Look at the recipe section for some tasty ideas.

Now let's go on to ways of familiarising children with fruit and vegetables.

10

GROWING FOOD

Non-gardeners welcome! No gardening skills are needed to be able to enjoy the activities in this chapter.

Indeed, you may find gardening with children easier than cooking. For one thing you get more chances of success: unlike cooking, when you would make only one pie or cake, in gardening you plant many seeds at a time, so at least some should grow!

There's another advantage: results are much less important.

If your peas produce only two or three pods, it doesn't matter two hoots. Children won't know this wasn't prize-winning gardening, but they will have seen how one pea can grow into many, and have learnt that peas come from pods on plants outdoors and not from plastic bags in the freezer. And, importantly, they will have tasted the incomparable flavour of fresh vegetables and fruit, so different from anything tinned or frozen.

But the reasons for growing things with children are very similar to those for cooking;

- it's fun
- it's creative
- it's educational
- it shows how good home-produced food can be!

It also a lovely way of enhancing a child's sense of wonder at the natural world. Watching a tiny seed develop into a plant does have that touch of magic about it.

You don't actually need a garden; you can start growing plants in the kitchen.

—— Growing things indoors ——

Start by sprouting seeds which is very easy. It's quick, too. You'll have something to eat in less than a week.

Sprouted seeds

Choose from chickpeas, alfalfa, mung beans, mustard seeds, green or yellow whole lentils and whole grains of wheat or oats. Buy them fresh as older ones may not sprout. Other seeds could be used too, but never sprout any seeds that are sold for planting, as they may have been treated with chemicals.

1 Grow about two tablespoonfuls at a time.
2 Pick them over first to remove any damaged ones or foreign bodies.
3 Put them in a sieve and rinse under the tap.
4 Tip them into a large, clean yogurt pot or something similar.
5 Cover well with water.
6 Cover lightly with the lid and leave overnight in a cool place.
7 Next day, tip the seeds into a sieve to drain off the water.
8 Rinse the seeds well under the cold tap and replace in the container.
9 Cover lightly again and once again leave overnight.
10 Each day, rinse the seeds under the tap, then replace in your covered container. They shouldn't smell musty, but if they do, rinse more often and drain more completely before replacing.

You'll have sprouts to eat within a week. How to eat them? Add them to salads, sandwiches, omelettes, soups, casseroles, or eat simply as finger-food nibbles.

Try gently toasting larger sprouted seeds like chickpeas in a spot of oil in a frying pan.

Mustard and cress

Another easy classic. It can hardly go wrong unless you let it dry out.

1 Take a small margarine or cottage cheese tub and poke drainage

holes through it all over the base. Put it on a plate and cover the bottom of the tub with a thick layer of cotton wool.
2   Sprinkle a few seeds on the cotton wool.
3   Water the seeds well.
4   Cover lightly with the lid.
5   Water the seeds morning and evening to keep them moist.
6   After the seeds have begun to sprout, leave them uncovered. Let the stalks grow tall, and when green leaves open you can harvest your crop! Scatter over salads, or eat with bread.

Humpty Dumpty Egg-shells

Grow the seeds on cotton wool in egg-shells. Waterproof inks or coloured pencils can be used to draw a face on the shell. Soon, Humpty will grow a shock of green hair!

Try other containers – sea shells look attractive, or you could make little floating islands by growing the seeds in coffee jar lids and floating them in a tray of water.

Sprouting avocado seeds

All seeds sprout roots and shoots, but it's difficult for children to see how it happens in a cluster of small seeds. Sprout some large seeds such as an avocado pear or broad beans. There won't be anything to eat here, just a biology demonstration.

1   Save an avocado stone. Wash it, then let it dry out. To avoid disappointment, start two or three stones as not all will grow.
2   Balance each seed on the top of a thin glass jar – the sort that are sold for growing hyacinths are ideal, but any jar that fits the seed will do.
3   Fill the jar up with water. Make sure the water touches the avocado seed.
4   Just wait two or three weeks for the seed to burst into life. It will be quite dramatic: it will split open vertically and a fat shoot will grow out, while roots grow into the water.
5   After the slow start, the new plant will grow rapidly and soon have large leaves.
6   If you want to keep the plant, it will need more nourishment, so plant it carefully into a large pot of compost. To get a bushy plant,

cut it back when it's as long as your hand. Otherwise let it shoot up and become a young tree. Keep it indoors in winter as frost will kill it.

Growing beans in jars

Try broad beans or large runner beans.

1 First choose a wide glass jar.
2 Soak the beans overnight to give them a good start.
3 Cut a piece of blotting paper or something similarly absorbent and coil it round the inside of the jar. As paper should closely touch the glass all the way round, it mustn't come up through the neck. If it overlaps itself quite a bit it will be stronger. Double thickness paper helps too.
4 Tip water round the jar to wet the paper and leave a drop in the bottom to keep the paper wet.
5 Gently push one or two beans half way down into the jar, trapping them between the paper and the glass.
6 Each day tip water round the jar to keep the paper wet and the atmosphere damp.
7 In a day or two, each bean will split open and a sturdy white root will grow out, followed by a green shoot, complete with tiny folded leaves.
8 Having observed the procedure, you could carefully transfer one of the beans to a pot of earth or compost, or plant it in the garden, and watch the whole plant grow. (Runner beans grow to human height at least, and will need a cane to climb up. Broad beans will need tying loosely to a short cane for support.)
Save at least one bean in the jar and see how the roots grow and branch out to show what the bean underground is doing.

Eventually the plants will produce flowers and then bean pods, and you will soon have home-grown beans to eat!

Comparing different roots

Each plant has its own type of root just as it has its own type of leaves and flowers. Sprout different kinds of seeds and notice their different roots.

1 Try a potato and an onion. Balance each on the top of a glass jar.
2 Pour water into the jars, but don't let it quite touch the vegetables or they may rot.
3 Wait for roots to grow. The potato may also grow stubby green shoots out of its 'eyes'. The green parts of potatoes are poisonous, so put the potato out of the reach of young children.
4 Compare the roots with the avocado's. If you sprout vegetables in the autumn you'll be able to compare them with the roots of any hyacinths growing in jars.

Sprouted vegetable tops

Not for eating, but easy to do:

1 Cut a thick slice (two to three centimetres) off the leaf end of some root vegetables, such as parsnip, beetroot, turnip, swede, celeriac and carrot. Stand the cut end in shallow water and wait for leaves to sprout. Notice the red beetroot leaves and the distinctive smell of the celeriac.
2 Children might like to make a tray garden with them, with stones and gravel between the plants.

What does a grapefruit tree look like?

Find out by planting some grapefruit seeds! In fact it's fun to plant all kinds of seeds, just to see what you get. Try apple, pear and citrus fruit pips; try whole blackberries, garlic cloves, parrot seed, brown rice, pot barley, wild rose-hips, chestnuts, tomato, chives, fennel and dill seeds, peach and plum stones – or anything else you want to try.

1 Wash the seeds first to get them started, then push small seeds just under some earth or compost in yogurt pots. Larger seeds can go in a little deeper.
2 Poke drainage holes in the bases of the pots or the seeds will rot.
3 Label each pot with the seed's name and the date it was planted.
4 Water the seeds from time to time but don't saturate them.

A little scientific experiment

Can the children make water go up – and stay up? Plants can! Right up to their topmost leaves.

Cut a stalk of celery and stand it in a glass containing a little ink, or water with a few drops of food colouring in. Next day children will be surprised to see what has happened to the celery!

Cut the celery stalk in half to see how it happened.

Windowsill herbs

Many herbs will thrive indoors. Just avoid very tall ones. Try chives, parsley, basil, thyme, golden marjoram, bay, mint, sage, lemon geranium, curry plant or rosemary.

- keep them in an light, airy place, but avoid leaving them in hot sun or they will scorch
- stand each pot on a saucer
- keep your plants in the right sized pots. Here's a test: tip each plant out of its pot. If you can see lots of roots then it's time to put the plant into a larger pot with more potting compost
- water herbs from the top. Keep them slightly moist but not sodden. To find out if a plant needs watering, pick it up! If it feels very light it needs water
- if you want the plants to thrive, buy some liquid plant food, dilute as directed on the label and feed the plants every ten days

Chives

Chives are the easiest herbs to grow. Either buy a plant or grow your own from seeds. Just keep them watered and snip off the blades as needed for garnish or putting in salads.

Parsley

Parsley too is easy if you buy a plant. It's unpredictable to grow from seed, and it takes weeks to germinate, although the flat-leaved sort is a little easier. Keep parsley watered and when using, cut off the stalks close to the soil. Use the stalks – they contain most of the flavour.

Parsley is a biennial, which means each plant will live two years. During the second year it will grow seeds and then die.

Basil

Basil is lovely to eat chopped up with tomatoes in summer. Buy a plant, not seeds and it will live a season in a sunny window.

Bay, Rosemary, Thyme and Sage

All these herbs will eventually grow too big for a windowsill. Meanwhile, cut them back, dry the leaves and store in jars in a cool place.

Mint

Mint doesn't like being confined, and will last only a season or two in a container. After that, plant it outside and let it spread its roots.

Rue

Rue is a pretty blue-green plant, but it's *poisonous* so don't have it just in case it gets nibbled.

Keeping herbs around enables children to become familiar with them, especially if you talk about them when you're using them. Show children how to rub their fingers on the leaves, smell their fingers and compare the different aromas left behind.

See if any cuttings will root in water. Cut a small piece off a plant and leave in a pot of water. Crush the stalk if it's woody so it can drink the water. If the cutting grows roots, then you have a new plant to grow! Another way to grow a cutting is to dip the end of the stem in water, then in hormone rooting powder and then plant it in a small pot of moist compost. It may grow better if you improvise a greenhouse by enclosing the whole pot in a clear plastic bag, and you won't need to water it. Show children how condensation forms on the inside of the bag and keeps the plant moist.

Buy a bag of 'multi-purpose' compost and use it for all your seeds, cuttings and plants.

You could plant all the above mentioned herbs in an outside window box, or in tubs or in the garden, but remember that basil will only last one sunny summer – it's a Mediterranean plant. Don't crowd the herbs as they need room to spread.

Windowboxes and tubs

Make sure that windowboxes are firmly secured or you could lose the lot. One way is to thread a piece of wire through the box and attach it to hooks inserted either side of the window.

- Provide for drainage. Tubs should have drainage holes, and small ones need 'plant saucers' to stand in so they don't dry out. Put a good layer of gravel or pebbles at the bottom of large tubs and windowboxes,
- Almost fill with all-purpose compost, not garden soil. Leave a three to four centimetre gap at the top to allow for watering.
- Put in any of the above mentioned herbs. Remember that in time some will grow large. Either omit those or trim them periodically.
- Thyme, chives, rosemary, borage and feverfew (get the prettier 'double' kind) have flowers.

Try strawberry or wild strawberry plants. If your tubs are large, try a potato plant for fun! Any of the plants mentioned on pages 91–2 can be grown in large containers. You can feed tubs with tomato fertiliser as directed on the container, but see also page 101.

HOW TO WATER

In summer, you'll need to water your containers every day it doesn't rain. Gently pour in water until some comes out of the bottom of the tub. That means the water has seeped right down and not just wet the top few centimetres.

Children can help at all stages: putting handfuls of compost into the tubs, digging holes where the plants will go, gently putting the plants in, putting the compost back round the plant until it's level, and then 'giving it a good drink'. Supervise everything well and perhaps share the work between you. Do explain, especially to small children, that plants can get hurt easily, just like people, and then they won't grow properly. Children can enjoy being gentle when they understand it's important.

Children could also plant a few seeds in the tubs. Nasturtiums are easy and will have lots of flowers throughout the summer. All parts of this plant are edible! English marigolds (with edible flowers) candytuft, honesty, Welsh poppies and Shirley poppies are also easy to grow. Keep the silvery seed pods of honesty for table decorations in winter. Encourage children to pick and arrange flowers with a bit of greenery for the dining table as part of their contribution to the meal.

TUB SAFETY

If you are going to have tubs on a patio where children play, choose carefully. Avoid:

- those built in sections and held together only by gravity
- any with rough or sharp edges
- pedestal-types, which are very easily knocked over

Go for smooth, rounded pots that are bottom-heavy. Plastic is kinder than stone when bumped into. You can improvise tubs out of a pile of old car tyres! Hide the sides with trailing plants such as variegated ivy, lobelia and nasturtiums.

Tomatoes

You can grow tomatoes in big pots of compost or in open ground. They need a bit of attention, but are worth it for the exquisitely delicious fruit. Buy either 'Gardeners' Delight' or 'Sweet 100'. They both have small fruit but the best flavour. Choose bushy plants, not long thin ones.

1   Choose your sunniest spot for tomato growing. Put each plant into an 8″ diameter pot or straight in the ground. If you're using a pot, put broken crocks or pebbles on the bottom for drainage, then fill up with all-purpose compost to five centimetres (two inches) below the rim. Firm the plant into place and water well. Tomatoes are thirsty things. The soil (or compost) must be kept moist. Letting the plants dry out and then soaking them is not the same thing.

2   Put a one and a half metre (four to five foot) sturdy cane close to the plant, but not so near that it cuts through its roots. As the

plant grows, you must tie it up at about 30 centimetres (one foot) intervals or you'll find the plant lying on the ground!

3 Pinch out all side shoots with thumb and finger as soon as you notice them. If you don't, they will grow quickly into big rival stems and rob the main plant of food. Similarly pull off any that start growing out at ground level. But the sap in tomato plants is *poisonous*, so *adults only* and wash your hands immediately afterwards.

4 Soon little yellow flowers will appear, followed by tiny green tomatoes. From then on, feed the tomatoes every week with a liquid tomato fertiliser; applied as directed on the label. (This type of fertiliser is also good for all kinds of other edible – and flowering – plants too!) Keep the container's child-proof top on and keep the container where no child can get to it.

And that's all. You can cut the top of the plant off if it gets too tall, or when four sprays ('trusses') of tomatoes have formed. After that, just enjoy picking the wonderful fruit.

Pick any green tomatoes that are left at the end of the season and ripen them on a sunny window-sill indoors, but away from a child's grasp: they can be *poisonous* if eaten under ripe.

─────────── **In the garden** ───────────

Herbs make wonderful edging plants. Try flowering thyme, purple sage, curry plant and golden marjoram.

Rocket and fennel are spectacularly tall plants, and easy to grow. Eat rocket in salads. Use fennel fronds to flavour fish dishes. Collect the masses of seeds from the umbrella-like seed heads in the autumn and save for flavouring.

Borage is a funny floppy plant with beautiful bright blue flowers. Freeze some of its flowers in ice cubes for children's summer drinks.

Sweet Cicely is useful in the garden as it comes into flower after the daffodils and when there's not much else out. It looks rather like hedge parsley and will grow anywhere including under trees. The leaves, when rubbed, smell of aniseed. Edible but unrewarding.

Growing easy vegetables

Before you plant anything, dig the soil over as deeply as you can, remove all weeds (don't dig them in!) and dig in some bonemeal and peat or peat substitute, following the instructions on the bags. Then chop the soil up finely. All this is strictly adult work. Do it in early spring. Plant seeds in the first warm weather after early March.

Get some marker pegs to indicate exactly where you have planted your seeds, and to say what they are!

Now you can involve children. Some vegetables are easier than others. Choose from the following list to start off with.

Potatoes

Potatoes are the easiest of all. Plant any potato that is beginning to sprout, though ideally, the sprouts should be a centimetre or so long. Plant them about 20 centimetres (eight inches) deep and about 60 centimetres (two feet) apart.

When leaves appear above the soil surface, pile soil around them in a mound. Keep doing this as the plant grows to keep the new baby potatoes in the dark. If any light catches them they will turn green. Green potatoes are *poisonous* as are the leaves. After about two months and after white flowers have appeared and died off you can carefully dig up the plant (with a fork if possible) and find all the new potatoes. See if you can find the one you planted, now wrinkled and shrunken, its work finished. You will now have seen the full life cycle of the plant. And how funny, to think of a potato as a seed! But that's what it is.

You can easily grow a potato plant in a tub, or an old bucket or even in a black plastic bag, indoors or out. Keep the earth moist but not wet.

Try an experiment to find out if potatoes know where the light is. Put a sprouted potato in a sealed box with a hole in one side. After a few weeks you could see the potato shoots coming through the hole!

Spinach

Spinach is also extremely easy and will grow almost anywhere. It's much less acidic to eat than the stuff you buy. Buy seeds called 'Spinach Beet' or 'Perpetual Spinach,' which will last through the winter. Just rub the seeds into the soil with your fingers. Baby leaves can be eaten raw in salads.

Radishes

These are often recommended for children to grow because they are ready for harvesting in just three or four weeks, but they do need some attention or they'll be hard and woody. They need a sunny spot. The soil must be kept damp. They must not be crowded or none will grow, so pull up those that are squashed together and discard. Eat with bread.

At the end of the season, leave one or two plants to grow tall, flower and develop seed pods. When the pods have turned brown and dry, pull up the plant, put it on a large sheet of newspaper and shake out all the seeds – all exactly like the ones you planted, and all ready to plant next spring. Children will now have seen the complete life cycle.

Broccoli

There is no comparison between broccoli on sale in shops and the utterly delicious kind you can grow so easily yourself. It takes a whole year to grow, but you can harvest it for about six weeks: it just keeps on coming! Buy 'sprouting broccoli', either yellow or purple. Buy either little plants in a box or sow your own seeds in compost in a shallow box or tray.

When the plants are about eight centimetres (two to three inches) high, plant them out in the garden and give them a good watering. They will grow huge, so leave nearly a metre between them. Water them in the evening for the first few weeks, and after that they should take care of themselves. Watch out for caterpillars and snails hiding in the leaves however, and pick them off. If lots of little white flies move in, spray them with liquid Derris, which is a natural, bio-degradable fly-killer.

Next spring, first cut the cauliflower-like head and then keep cutting all the little sprouts that will grow lower down. Later, the plants will burst into bright yellow flower! At this point, pull them and discard them. But if you want see the whole life cycle, leave one plant in the ground. The flowers will die and leave tiny pods behind, all full of seeds. Save these if you like, when they have become brown and ripe.

Runner beans

Plant beans in little pots of compost, keep slightly damp only – if the compost gets too wet the beans will rot. In about a fortnight, you will have strong little plants each with two big leaves. At this point, plant them out in the garden or in a large tub, with a long cane by each plant for it to climb up. Make a wigwam of canes for strength.

Keep runner beans well-watered. If you see any tiny black flies on the plants, especially underneath the leaves, wipe them off with wet fingers. Spray the flies with water into which you've put (only) one or two drops of washing-up liquid. (Too much will kill the plant.)

Measure their progress as the beans climb to the tops of their poles. Soon the plants will be covered with red flowers. After this, watch the flowers die, leaving behind tiny bean pods. Harvest the pods when they are about 15 centimetres (six inches) long. They will taste exquisite.

Leave a few pods on the plants to grow huge and hard and to turn brown and dry. Pick them, crack them open and see all the big pink beans inside, just like the ones which were planted. Save them for planting next year. You can now have free runner beans forever!

Peas

Poke dried pea-seeds into the soil, about 1 centimetre deep and about eight centimetres (three inches) apart. Either plant them in a little group, or, if you're more ambitious, plant a row of them. The usual way is to plant three rows of peas next to each other, the rows eight centimetres (three inches) apart:

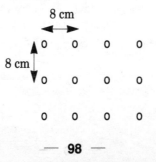

Pea plants are too weak to support themselves, so surround them with sticks or, better still, very twiggy twigs. The plants will grow tiny tendrils that will fasten on tightly to the twigs. After white, butterfly-like flowers have grown and died, you will see minute pea pods. Harvest them in two or three weeks when they have filled out but are still young and sweet. The flavour is indescribably good. Eat at least some of them raw, they're almost too good to cook!

As with beans, leave a few pods to grow fat, ripen and dry on the plants. Save for planting next year.

Fruit

Try some fruit too. There's nothing like an apple picked straight off the tree. You can buy miniature apple trees in tubs, but it's lovely to have a full-sized tree in the garden. If there are no other apple trees close by, you must get one that's self-fertile – and then go for flavour, such as the new self-fertile Cox's Orange Pippin. If you never spray your tree, the apples may have maggots in them and won't keep long, but that might not be a problem to you.

Redcurrants

Redcurrants must be the easiest fruit to grow of all. Simply buy a bush, plant in well-dug soil into which you've put bonemeal and peat or peat substitute, and wait for it to grow about a metre in height and width and be covered in sprays of luscious jewel-like fruit. Pick them before the birds do! Protect the fruit by putting an old net curtain or some plastic green mesh over the plants. Notice the delicate yellow-green flowers that come before the fruit.

Children can easily help to pick the sprays. Eat them by dipping each spray of currants in a little sugar and then pull the currants off with your teeth. Eat with bread as a perfect summer snack. Redcurrants bushes need no pruning, unlike blackcurrants.

Raspberries

Another wonderful summer treat. So expensive to buy, you can have masses for free, year after year. Simply buy a few raspberry canes and tie them up to a fence or anything where they will have plenty of light and space. During the year, the canes will grow tall and need tying up. Small white flowers will appear, and then the fruit. Again, protect the fruit from birds.

When all the fruit is finished, cut down the brown canes close to ground level, being careful to save the new green ones for bearing fruit next year. Tie them up securely.

Blackberries

Blackberries are easy to grow too, but horribly thorny unless you buy a thornless kind. Again, tie the briars up to a support and in the autumn cut down all but the main briars. It can be fun for children – and adults – to 'go blackberrying'.

Wild strawberries

Wild strawberries will grow anywhere and spread rapidly. Easy for very young children to pick.

Teach children they must pick berries *only* when a familiar adult says they can. Explain that although some berries may look beautiful but are very bad to eat and can make you very, very ill. Teach them always to ask before they pick any kind of plant.

Giant sunflowers

These spectacular plants must have a place somewhere! Amazing it is for young children to see how such a tiny seed can grow into a flower plant much taller than even the adults! Pull it up at the end of the season, eat any seeds that the birds didn't get and exclaim how long the stalk is as it lies on the ground.

Their patch

As adults are in charge of all these activities, young children may yearn for their own patch of garden where they are in charge. Do make this available if they're interested. If all they want to do is make a 'play garden' with pebbles and sticks, or just enjoy digging with a trowel and pouring water on, let them do it. Make sure they're suitably clad and don't complain that they're not, in adult eyes, doing anything useful. If they ask to help, try to offer them something other than weeding to do – it's been known to put people off for life!

Garden safety

Garden tools can cause horrific accidents. Here are a few rules:

1 **Never** lay tools down on the ground: they don't show up well and can so easily be tripped over. Push your spade or fork firmly into the ground the moment you stop using it. And paint your tools a bright colour so they are easily seen.
2 **Never** leave secateurs or shears open.
3 **Never** leave the garden rake propped up with prongs facing outwards – and hang it up immediately you've finished with it.
4 Keep young children indoors while you use electrical tools. **Never** leave them unattended, just in case.
5 Take special care when using fertilisers, weed-killers and such. Keep all such things in their original containers, sealed and always out of reach of any child.
6 When you finish for the day (or session), lock everything away securely.

11

PARTIES, PICNICS AND OUTINGS

Festive events such as birthdays have traditionally been times of good eating. Most cultures save their choicest foods for days of celebration.

Extraordinary, then, that nowadays when we want to celebrate a happy event like a child's birthday we so often serve salty, greasy packet-snacks, highly coloured sweets, sugary cake and fake orange juice. By providing such fare, we train children to think of junk food as a 'treat', and the proper thing for parties.

One disadvantage of the usual high-sugar-and-additive commercial 'party' food is children can become extremely 'high' on it. Many parents have seen their children become quite impossible after a party, way beyond normal party excitement.

It's not difficult to make delicious, party-ish food from ordinary good ingredients. A lot depends on presentation: it's essential that the table looks special, so that the children exclaim when they first see it; the food should have variety and colour, and look fun and easy to eat. Touches of humour are essential.

Setting the scene

Buy a long strip of any brightly coloured fabric and call that your 'party tablecloth'. It will set off everything you put on it. Or buy a special paper 'party' cloth. Putting a sheet of plastic underneath takes the worry out of spills.

- for fun — and to save on breakages and washing up — use paper or plastic plates and bowls
- coloured, bendy drinking straws are fun, and fancy paper napkins are pretty, and handy for small spills
- add any other fripperies that you fancy such as coloured streamers, party hats, funny place names, crackers and so on. Bunches of balloons hung near the table add to the atmosphere
- you could have a 'themed' table setting to match your child's current interest
- the table should look inviting even without any food!

Present the food well

It is best to provide plates holding lots of small pieces of food that can be picked up easily. Avoid food that needs cutting up. Make sure children can reach different kinds of food without stretching and leaning over.

- aim for food in a variety of shapes and sizes
- serve some food on silver platters! Just cover plates or trays with crumpled cooking foil
- cover flat plates and chopping boards with red or gold shiny paper. Fasten down well with sticky tape. Or use pretty wrapping paper covered with cling film
- aim for each plate of food to be colourful, either the food itself or some edible garnish
- give some height to the display — perhaps a tall cake stand, pots of commercial bread sticks or celery sticks, or some fancy centrepiece you've devised!

Party food ideas

Most of the food should be savoury. Many children prefer this and they'll feel better for it afterwards. Do have the savoury food ready on the table so the children will have something to do immediately they sit down. Sandwiches are the obvious idea and they're fine – but make them interesting, and make some double-decker and open-faced ones too.

In general, go for ideas that you know you can put together fairly quickly. Don't over-cater: it's easily done. There doesn't have to be masses of food.

Double-decker sandwiches

Alternate brown and white bread in each sandwich. Cut into rectangles, squares and triangles. Have either the same filling or two different fillings:

- curd cheese with sunflower seeds, slices of avocado in lemon juice and tomato strips and cress
- curd cheese and slices of avocado in lemon juice, tuna and tomato slices
- shredded lettuce and tiny, thin carrot sticks with sardines mashed in lemon juice
- cold scrambled or hard-boiled egg mashed with a speck of mayonnaise, with cress or shredded lettuce
- chopped prawns with a speck of mayonnaise with shredded lettuce and chopped celery
- cheddar cheese with any salad items and sprouted sunflower seeds
- soft herb cheese with paper-thin slices of cucumber. (Why is it that lots of thin slices of cucumber taste so much nicer then a few thick ones?)
- home-made 'fish paste' (see recipe on page 176) with lettuce
- peanut butter or tahini with sesame seeds and a little good quality honey.

No need to butter the bread first when the fillings are tasty and moist.

Open-faced sandwiches

These are faster to make, and simple ones can be assembled very quickly: with these, children can see exactly what they're getting. Make them on bread or toast shapes, cheese scones, baps, crispbreads, matzos or crackers. Four ideas are:

1 Spread with curd cheese, herb cheese, peanut butter or mashed, cooked egg. If you have time, you can put on one or two toppings.

Just a halved, seedless black grape on top of chopped egg looks eye-catching. You could use cold, cooked tomato sauce (see recipe on page 156) as a bright red spread.

2 Make faces on some of them: make two large eyes and a smiley or glum mouth. Use sultanas, tomato strips, diamonds of red or green peppers, tufts of cress and pieces of carrot for making faces or other designs.

3 Make traffic lights: spread half a bap with curd cheese or cooked eggs, then use red, yellow and green peppers for the lights, cutting them with an apple corer or a small pastry cutter.

4 Make bap boats: spread half a bap with curd cheese or cooked egg, then cut a triangular sail from a red pepper. Or use sticks of carrot and celery for funnels on a steamboat.

For very special effects, use a little lumpfish – the black colour is so striking. Alternatively, halved, seeded black grapes are useful for colour contrast.

Pinwheels

Flatten a slice of de-crusted bread a little by rolling with a rolling pin. Cover with a thin layer of any spreadable filling and roll up. Repeat with a few other slices of bread and chill, packed together in the fridge until needed. Then, slice into pinwheels and arrange on a plate.

One bite open sandwiches

Make these on cheese biscuits, or stamp out small, thick circles of bread with a pastry cutter. Also make them on thick slices of cucumber, or on carrot or celeriac slices. Put on any soft cheese as 'glue', then decorate with one or two items:

Try a twist of cucumber, ham or mortadella, a slice of tomato, a posy of mustard-and-cress, a tuft of finely-grated carrot soaked in orange juice with raisins, a criss-cross of thin red-pepper strips, a piece of sardine, tuna, salmon or pilchard, a blob of taramasalata, or just a dusting of bright red paprika.

Biting baps

Slice baps three-quarters of the way through. Push some frilly lettuce inside, along with a slice of soft cheese, or cheese and ham, or pieces of tuna, sardine or pilchard, so that the bap looks like an open mouth filled with food.

Dipsticks and dips

Arrange little bunches of neatly cut vegetable sticks on brightly coloured plates, and 'tie' each bunch with a chive blade or a curly strip of pepper. Stand longer ones in decorated beakers. Some red pepper, green pepper and carrot are musts, for their strong colour.

Try other sticks such as yellow and orange peppers, cheese, breadsticks, celery, celeriac, cucumber, courgette.

Try one or two dips such as: hummus (see page 177), Greek yogurt or curd cheese beaten with milk (perhaps coloured pink with tomato puree or beetroot, or liquidised with watercress or parsley to turn it pale green).

Filling the gaps

Empty spaces on serving plates make food look less inviting, so fill in the gaps!

Use baby tomatoes, radishes, radish 'roses', spring onion tassels, cauliflower and broccoli 'trees', black grapes, dried apricots, dates, pieces of pineapple, satsuma segments, watercress sprigs and so on. Try a few edible flowers: English marigolds, chives, courgette or nasturtium. Remember all garnishes must be edible, as someone is bound to try them!

Make an attractive border round the edge of a dish with halved lemon or orange slices.

Make a criss-cross pattern over food with chive blades or strips of cucumber peel; or use them to depict a noughts-and-crosses game, with cucumber slices for the noughts! Try this on a plate of yogurt or curd cheese dip.

Sweet dishes

There doesn't have to be a trifle, but if you want one there's a reasonably harmless party trifle recipe on page 166. Or try the luscious and entirely beneficial Terrine des Fruits on page 166, or Apricot jelly crunch on page 169. You can serve these from a large bowl or make them in individual dishes.

After that, children may be ready for only a few more sweet nibbles. You really don't need to have any cakes as such, but if you want to make one, look at page 180 before you start. For a sweet taste to end the meal, try some of the following:

1　Have a plate of dried fruits such as apple rings, pear slices, apricots. Decorate with large seeded raisins.
2　Arrange lots of orange or thin, apple slices in concentric circles on a plate. Cover with cling film and keep in the fridge until needed. (Toss the apple slices in a little lemon juice first to stop them browning.)
3　Scatter pieces of various fruits on a plate and prepare as above. Choose from de-pipped black grapes, bunchlets of three to four seedless green or red grapes, seedless satsuma segments, thick, diagonal banana slices dipped in lemon, kiwi fruit slices and pineapple pieces. In summer, add slices of peach and nectarine, blackberries, redcurrants and so on.
4　Make some 'fruit cushions': place a whole strawberry (or raspberry, clementine segment, kiwi fruit or mango slice, or any other special treat) on a cushion of cream cheese on a small square of bread, sugar-free oatcake or shortbread biscuit. Allow at least one per child plus a few spares. These look amazingly good arranged on a large 'silver' platter (see page 103).

———— The birthday cake ————

Every birthday party must have a candle-lighting ceremony but that doesn't mean a cake is compulsory: any food would do that will accommodate birthday candles and a cake-frill.

Alternatively, fix some medium-sized candles firmly onto a plate with plasticine – or playdough – and cover the plasticine and plate with crumpled cooking foil, making holes for the candles to poke through.

If you use a large plate for this, you could surround the candles with some 'fruit cushions' (see above) to be handed round after the candles are blown out.

On the other hand, if you can't have cake on your birthday, when can you! If you wish to make one yourself so you know what's in it, look at page 180.

—————————— Drinks ——————————

Mix your own to avoid all the sugar, artificial sweeteners and other additives in the mass-produced kinds. Try:

- diluted genuine fruit juice – orange, apple, pineapple or mixed juices
- milk for young children as a choice
- nursery fruit cup: dilute concentrated pear juice and add enough lemon juice for a home-made lemonade flavour. Serve it from a jug or from a glass bowl with a ladle. On the top, you could float pieces of fruit or ice cubes containing fruit or edible flowers
- in cold weather, serve the above drink hot. Delicious for children or adults
- have a jug of water to offer as a choice – but not bottled mineral water as some makes have too many minerals in for children

You can have quite a feast that will satisfy the hungriest party boy or girl. Don't be surprised or hurt if at least one child doesn't want to eat much. It's not uncommon and it's not your fault. If the child looks unhappy, try to see what the matter is – perhaps he can't reach the only item of food he really wants and is too shy to ask. In any case, don't make a fuss about it and embarrass the child, who may simply prefer not to eat at that moment.

————— Picnics and outings —————

If you take your own, home-prepared picnic food, your children will be on familiar ground and you'll be in control of what they're getting.

- salt and sugar create thirst, so avoid these in picnic food and drink. Take plenty of ordinary water to drink — and plastic beakers to drink it out of

- a cool-bag or box will keep food and water cold for hours
- take thirst-quenching food such as cucumber, celery and fresh fruit
- take food which will stand up to a bit of punishment – apples will survive better than soft pears; bread rolls survive better than slices
- wrap everything individually so you can undo things one at a time and hand things out bit by bit
- take plenty of paper napkins for a multitude of uses — and don't forget a first-aid kit

If you intend to eat out, you might want to take a few staples such as fresh fruit, plain biscuits, dried fruit, and perhaps some good fruit bread in case you strike unlucky. 'Children's menus' in so many places are just fry-ups and ice-cream.

Even if the food is good, there's no guarantee your children will want to eat it. All kinds of things can put children off, and if you have some emergency rations, you won't need to worry. (If the children's menu is appalling, try to have the courage to complain quietly to the manager, although the answer will probably be that everybody else likes it! The answer to that is that very few people think it's worth complaining about something which is so commonly poor … But don't get into an argument that ruins your outing.)

If the food is good, do compliment the staff. We heard of a Scottish restaurant which took the trouble to make smiley faces with bits of tomato on the children's baked potatoes – such a simple thing and yet so much appreciated by both children and their parents.

And baby comes too?

Babies can find long outings very stressful, and it can be difficult to keep a baby cool and content whilst travelling, so unless your picnic spot is close to home, it might be better to postpone such trips until a little later.

If you have to travel with your baby, take plain boiled water, plus a supply of whatever milk or food she is used to, perhaps packed in a cool-bag. This isn't the moment to switch suddenly to bought baby food if she's not used to it: it may be spat out. If you're using formula milk, remember you can get it in single portion containers; they're convenient and you don't have to worry about keeping them cool. To take the chill off milk, you can put the bottle under your arm!

Foodie outings

With older children, you could have a food-related outing, especially if you live in a city or have no garden. A visit to a working windmill, a pick-your-own fruit and vegetable farm, a horticultural college, a stately home with a vegetable garden or orchard, or just a walk round some local allotments or garden centre can be interesting and instructive – for adults too!

All in all, keep food on the agenda and keep it fun.

Part Two

RECIPES

12

WEANING RECIPES: FOUR TO FIVE MONTHS OLD

Abbreviations:

tsp.	=	teaspoon
tbl.	=	tablespoon
g	=	gram
ml	=	millilitre

Stage one: the first month of weaning

First read page 17 on 'How to wean a baby'.

These are examples of the very first 'solid' foods you could give your baby. They're not meals, just tastes, to let babies know there is more to mealtimes than mere milk!

These recipes will probably provide enough variety for your baby for the first two weeks of weaning. Remember it saves work to make up larger quantities and freeze in ice-cube trays for using later. Thaw one or two at a time as needed.

JUST A TASTE IN THE FIRST TWO WEEKS
Offer your baby tiny amounts, at first on your fingertip, and then later on the tip of a small, shallow plastic teaspoon.

BABY RICE

You can make this by sieving cooked rice and mixing in a little baby milk or breast milk. Alternatively you can buy packets of powdered baby rice from chemists and supermarkets – but check the ingredients list as some companies add extra sugar and flavouring agents which won't help your baby develop a taste for savoury foods. Stir baby rice into a little warm breast or formula milk and use straight away.

FRUITY RICE PORRIDGE

As above, but instead of adding all milk, add a little water from cooking an apple or pear – see Pear and Apple Purée. Or save a little of the fruit purée to stir into the porridge.

This simple variation can be an exciting new flavour for a baby, and an introduction to stronger fruit flavours.

PEAR PURÉE

1 Peel and core a ripe pear. Cut into thin slices and cook slowly in a small saucepan in a few tablespoons of previously boiled water, until completely cooked.
2 Remove the pieces of pear.
3 Boil the cooking water until it has reduced to about one tablespoonful.
4 Purée the pear with the cooking water.

PEARS

Buying ripe pears is tricky. One solution is to buy unblemished, sound-looking pears and ripen them at home. You can then choose 'the very moment' for using them.

To ripen pears: leave them to ripen slowly, unwrapped, in a cool, airy place. To test for ripeness: press the stalk end gently – it should feel soft. The rest of the pear should be very slightly soft. The best pears will have a faint but tempting aroma.

Use Comice or William pears rather than Conference, which can be very hard. In summer, look for red-skinned pears, which are particularly good.

APPLE PURÉE

1 Use a sweet dessert apple, not a cooker. Make sure it's ripe: if the pips are not dark brown then the apple is unripe and not suitable for a baby.
2 Peel and core a small ripe eating apple and cut into thin slices.
3 Simmer them slowly in a few tablespoons of boiled water until completely soft.
4 Remove the apple. Reduce the cooking water to about one table-spoonful by boiling fast.
5 Purée the apple with the cooking water.

CARROT PURÉE

Carrot purées come out bright orangy-red and always look exciting. Serve them to adults too as something different!

1 Scrub a small carrot and cut it into thin slices, put into a small saucepan, cover with boiled water, put on the lid, and simmer gently until soft. Remove the carrot.
2 Reduce the cooking water to a teaspoonful or so by boiling it fast. Replace the carrot in the water and purée.

CREAMY PURÉES

Mix any of the above purées with a little baby milk. You may prefer to introduce your baby to fruit by mixing it with milk to make it a more familiar flavour.

For a thicker purée use less liquid or add baby rice.

BABY JACKET

When you are cooking potatoes-in-their-jackets for the rest of the family, mash about a teaspoonful of well-cooked potato with a little baby milk to a smooth cream.

A LITTLE BIT MORE IN THE SECOND TWO WEEKS

Gradually give your baby more purées to try. To avoid confusing your baby and putting him off; offer no more than one new purée a day, and no more than three new ones a week.

BANANA MASH

Bananas are ripe when their skins are covered with black speckles. Give your baby only very ripe bananas as these are sweeter and easier to digest.

Mash a small amount of very ripe banana with a fork until completely smooth and almost liquid.

BANANA RICE PORRIDGE

Mash some very ripe banana as above. Combine in any proportion with Baby Rice on page 114.

PAPAYA

An expensive treat, yes, but papaya is a perfect baby food: it has a smooth texture, delicious sweet taste, bright colour – and useful nutrients. It needs to be cooked lightly for babies under six months.

1　Halve a ripe papaya lengthways and scoop out the pink flesh, discarding the black seeds.
2　Cut into small chunks and steam over boiling water for up to five minutes. Purée.

VEGETABLES FROM THE FAMILY POT

The easiest way to cook vegetables for a baby is simply to purée a small amount of those you've cooked for the family. But:

- remove the baby's portion before adding any seasoning
- cut vegetables into smaller pieces than you probably would normally do so they will cook more quickly and taste fresher
- when cooking green vegetables for a very young baby, make sure they are cooked quite soft

However, here are a few other ideas for cooking vegetables that are suitable for babies under six months old. Remember, it saves a lot of time if you cook large amounts and freeze in ice-cube trays.

HOW TO PURÉE

You don't have to have fancy equipment. Here are some ideas. You could use:

- a fork to mash soft foods such as banana and potato
- a sieve and a large spoon or, for larger amounts, it will be much easier to use the end of a very well scrubbed (handle-less!) rolling pin
- a potato masher, sometimes in conjunction with a sieve
- a hand-blender, which is convenient for puréeing very small amounts
- a Mouli-sieve, which comes with three different bases to give a choice of three different textures from fine to coarse. Cheaper to buy than an electric blender, it also has the advantage of automatically sieving out pips and skins. But it's metal, so it should be put in a warm place to get completely dry after you've washed it
- an ordinary electric blender is useful only for larger quantities or for very thin purées because of the difficulty of scraping the food out from around the blades

BROCCOLI PURÉE

1 Divide the broccoli into small florets. Make cuts in the thicker stalks for even cooking.
2 Either steam, or cook gently in boiling water until tender. The tip of a knife will slide easily into the thickest part of the stalk when the broccoli is done.
3 Purée with a little of the cooking water.

CAULIFLOWER PURÉE

Prepare and cook as for broccoli.

BROCCOLI AND CAULIFLOWER PURÉE

Cook florets of both together as for broccoli, above, then purée.

BABY MILK

In these recipes, 'baby milk' means either expressed breast milk or formula milk. No other type of milk should be used for babies under six months old.

BROCCOLI AND POTATO CREAM

1 Scrub a small potato and remove any blemishes. Cut into quarters. Cook gently in boiling water in a small, covered saucepan, then strain and peel. (Or scoop out the well-cooked inside of a jacket potato.)
2 Cook a few florets of broccoli as described above. Purée with the potato. Add as much baby milk as needed to make a smooth cream suitable for your baby.

VARIATION: substitute cauliflower for broccoli.

PARSNIP PURÉE

1 small parsnip
a pinch cinnamon

1 Scrub and peel a small parsnip, removing any tap roots and blemishes. Slice thinly.
2 Cover with boiled water in a small saucepan, put on the lid and simmer gently until the outer part of each slice is soft.
3 Remove from the water. Cut into chunks, cutting away and discarding the centre of each slice as you go. Purée the parsnip with a drop of cooking water if needed. Add a pinch of cinnamon.

ROOT VEGETABLE PURÉE

1 medium-sized potato
2 medium-sized slices of parsnip
2 carrots

1 Scrub the vegetables, removing any blemishes
   Cut the potato into about six pieces, slice the carrot thinly and put all three vegetables into a small saucepan with enough boiling water to cover.

2 Put on the lid; cook gently until all the vegetables are soft. Take the vegetables out of the water and slip the skins off the potato pieces.
3 Purée the vegetables with two or three teaspoons of their cooking water. You could freeze extra portions at this point.

VARIATION: Add a little baby milk just before serving.

BABY BEVERAGE

Always save the water that your baby's vegetables have been cooked in. Keep it in the fridge and use it for cooking the next day's vegetables for added flavour – it's good vegetable stock! All vegetables lose minerals and vitamins into their cooking water so it really is a pity to pour it down the drain.

You can also use it, diluted if necessary, as a delicious and nutritious drink. Boil it up well, perhaps with added water, then give it either warm or (not too) cold.

– Stage two: five to six months old –

AVOCADO PEAR

A ripe avocado will mash easily with a fork. Discard any lumps and any brownish or stringy bits.

Use straightaway before it turns brown.

FRUITY AVOCADO

1 Prepare the avocado and mash smoothly as above.
2 Then mix in a teaspoon or two of the water that fruit has been cooked in. Try apple, pear, peach, nectarine, apricot and plum. Boil the water fast to reduce it to a teaspoon or so. Alternatively, simply mash some banana into the avocado!

PEACHES AND BANANA

1 Use only very ripe peaches. They should ripen at home on a sunny windowsill if they're not quite ready when you buy them.
2 Wash them, then put them into hot water for a minute or so to loosen the skin. Rinse in a sieve under the cold tap then peel. If

the skin is hard to remove, replace the peach in the hot water for a little longer.

3 Put the peaches in a saucepan and just cover with boiling water. Simmer until cooked through, about five minutes, depending on ripeness.

4 Carefully take out the peaches, stone and slice roughly. Boil the cooking liquid fast until you have only one tablespoon per fruit. Purée the peach slices in this sweet liquid along with a some banana.

5 If the purée is made slightly runny, it makes a delicious and versatile sauce for serving with other fruit, or, for older babies, with egg custard.

VARIATION: try with other stone fruits in season: nectarines, apricots, and various types of plums.

GOLDEN APRICOT AND BANANA PUDDING

¹/₂ a large, ripe banana
120 g (4 oz) dried apricots*

1 Clean the apricots by pouring boiling water over them in a sieve. Soak them for a few hours or overnight in two teacups of cold water. Then tip the apricots and their soaking water into a small saucepan, put on the lid and cook very slowly for 40 minutes.

2 Purée with the banana.

For older babies, purée the apricots and mix with roughly mashed banana.

* To use non-soak apricots: after cleaning them, throw in fast boiling water, lower the heat to a simmer and proceed with the recipe.

GREEN BEAN PURÉE

1 Use either French beans or runner beans. Wash, top and tail and string them as needed. Slice thinly, diagonally.

2 Boil gently in water or vegetable stock for about five minutes or until just tender. Alternatively, steam them for slightly longer. Don't overcook them or they will turn grey and smell unpleasant.

3 Purée and sieve.

HOW TO WASH AND PREPARE LEEKS

To clean each leek thoroughly: split in half almost down to the root and wash well under the cold tap, holding the leek upside down and splaying out the layers under the water to wash out all soil and grit. Gritty-tasting leeks are very unpleasant to eat, but you can avoid this just by washing them properly.

LEEK CREAM

Leeks are tasty and sweet. They are good mixed with all kinds of vegetables. For young babies use only the white part.

50 g (2 oz) white part of a leek
³/₄ cup of baby milk
2 tsp. baby rice

Clean the leek. Cut into very thin slices and simmer until tender in milk, (about eight minutes). Purée with the milk, then sieve. Mix with a little baby rice.

VARIATION: Cook the leek in a mixture of baby milk and vegetable stock.

LEEKS AND GREEN BEANS

1 Wash the leeks thoroughly as above. Cut a few thin slices from the white part.
2 Wash, top and tail the beans and string as necessary. Cut diagonally into thin slices.
3 Cook the leeks in a little boiling vegetable stock for two minutes, then add the beans. Cook gently for about five minutes until just tender. Purée and sieve.

SWEET POTATO

1 Scrub and peel a sweet potato and remove any blemishes.
2 Cut into smallish chunks and boil in plain water for about 20 minutes or until completely tender, then purée or mash.

Sweet potatoes do taste sweet. You can emphasise this by adding a little mashed banana to the purée!

CARROT AND LENTIL SOUP

about 50 g (2 oz) carrot
30 g (1 oz) small red lentils
50 g (2 oz) the white part of a leek
baby milk to serve

1 First cook the lentils: bring two teacups of water to the boil in a smallish saucepan. Pick over the lentils, and wash in a sieve under the cold tap. Drain, then throw into the fast-boiling water. Skim as the water comes back to the boil and then boil rapidly for ten minutes. Lower the heat and simmer for another ten minutes, stirring towards the end until the lentils are have absorbed the water and become a soft mass.
2 Meanwhile, scrub the carrot and slice thinly. Clean the leek as above and cut thin slices from the white part.
3 Simmer the carrot and leek together with a teacupful of water (or vegetable cooking water) in a small, covered saucepan until soft (about ten minutes).
4 Purée the lentils with the carrot and leek. Just before using, thin as needed with baby milk.

13

RECIPES FOR BABIES FROM SIX TO EIGHT MONTHS OLD

You can now add many different foods to your baby's repertoire: purées of chicken, turkey and liver, well-cooked egg-yolk, all types of lentils and small beans such as aduki, foods containing wheat, certain vegetables such as spinach, turnips and swede, soft summer fruit and citrus fruit.

Please read page 24 on the subject of which type of milk is best. In this section, there are some recipes with small amounts of dairy foods such as yogurt and cheese. If you don't wish to give any milk products until after twelve months, just save the recipes containing these until later.

BABY BREAKFAST CEREAL

Quick and easy to prepare – and, unlike the bought kind, it can be tailor-made for your own baby.

rolled oats (organic have more taste)
crumbled Weetabix
wheatgerm or oatgerm
ripe banana
milk

Mix in any proportions with enough milk to purée it all easily. Serve as it is or with full-cream yogurt.

VARIATION: You could use this as a base for cereal for all the family. Add chopped nuts, sultanas or raisins, sunflower seeds, apple slices, yogurt and so on as you wish.

WHEATGERM AND MILK

Instant hot breakfast! And good for all children. When you buy wheatgerm, look for the sort with larger flakes which seem to taste sweeter than tiny flakes.

Stir the wheatgerm into hot milk to make a porridge.

VARIATION: you could make it sweeter still by puréeing (and sieving) sultanas in the milk beforehand.

BABY OATMEAL

'fine' oatmeal
baby milk
a little banana

1 Buy what is called 'fine' oatmeal and soak a handful overnight in enough boiled, cooled water to cover completely allowing a little extra water on top.
2 Next day, gently cook the oatmeal, stirring all the time. As the porridge thickens, dilute it with baby milk to soften and sweeten it.
3 Just before serving, add a little well mashed banana.

CHICKEN SOUP

Good home-made chicken soup is one of the delights of life. It's also a good introduction to the taste of meat. Make this recipe in quantity, freeze in small portions and use as stock, gravy or as delicious baby soup. Don't think of omitting the garlic! When cooked for a long time, garlic is soft, mild – and odourless! And it is very good with chicken.

1 good-sized boiling fowl,
cut into pieces
giblets and feet of the fowl
(but not the liver which gives
a bitter taste)
1 large onion, sliced
1 large carrot, scrubbed, sliced
2 outer stalks of celery,
scrubbed and sliced

a few cloves of garlic
chopped roughly
1 flat tsp. of dried thyme
a few parsley stalks
pinch of sage
a blade of mace OR pinch of
powdered mace
3-4 black peppercorns
a little olive oil

1 Brown the chicken pieces and giblets in hot oil in a large frying pan. Do them in two or three batches so as not to crowd them.

Turn with two wooden spoons to brown all over.

2   Transfer the browned pieces to a casserole dish or heavy saucepan as you do them.

3   Add the vegetables to the frying pan and toss over heat for 2-3 minutes.

4   Replace the chicken and cover completely with water. (*If you've browned the meat, boil up some water in the pan to remove the wonderful flavours, and add it the chicken.) Add the thyme, parsley, sage, peppercorns and mace and bring to the boil. Lower the heat, cover, and simmer slowly in the oven or on the top for 2-4 hours or until the chicken meat is thoroughly cooked: it depends on the size of the fowl. A large, 7 lb bird will take all of four hours, while a 4 lb one may be done within two.

5   Allow to cool a little, then strain. Put the chicken pieces to drain in a colander over a bowl. Discard the now very overcooked vegetables; this may sound wasteful, but they've given up their best taste and nutrients in the long cooking and have little value now for a baby.

6   When the stock has cooled sufficiently, put into the fridge. Next day, remove the layer of white fat and discard. Freeze the delicious jellied stock in small amounts.

*VARIATION: you can omit browning the meat and vegetables by putting everything into the pot with the water. The stock will have slightly less flavour and colour but still be good.

Using the meat and carcass

● remember that breastmeat cooks more quickly than the rest, so remove it about half through the cooking time before it gets tough and stringy

● purée a little meat with some stock to make a thick soup. As a variation, add a splash of milk just before using

● purée some chicken meat with any vegetable purée on pages 117 and 118. You could cook the vegetables in chicken stock instead of water

● older babies and toddlers could have slivers of chicken as finger food

● use the meat in meals for the rest of the family. Ready-cooked chicken is useful for salads, sandwiches and pilaffs. Try the chicken pie recipe on page 162.

● wrap in small parcels any meat you can't use at the moment and freeze

You can make excellent soup from the carcass of a roast chicken. Boil it up for about an hour with the flavourings listed above (onion, carrot, celery, thyme, sage, parsley, bay-leaf and peppercorns). But don't mix cooked and uncooked bones or the flavour and colour will be poor.

CHICKEN LIVER PURÉE

Use chicken stock to flavour baby's first taste of liver.

1/2 carton frozen chicken livers (115 g, 4 oz), thawed
150 ml (1/4 pint) chicken stock
1 tbl. potato mashed with milk

1   Heat the stock in a small saucepan.
2   Meanwhile, roughly chop the livers, removing fat and any other white bits and pieces as you go. Drop them into the boiling stock, stir round, lower the heat, cover, then leave to simmer slowly, stirring occasionally until done, about 10 minutes.
3   The livers are ready when they have just stopped being pink inside. Cooking too long will make them tough.
4   Purée with the potato.

VARIATION: Puréed green beans or peas go well with liver. You could have them as a separate dish or purée the whole lot together.

LIVER AND TOMATO DINNER

1 carton frozen chicken livers (227 g, 8 oz), thawed
1 small onion, chopped finely
1 tbl. olive oil
1 bay-leaf
2-3 Italian plum tomatoes (tinned)
*1/2 tsp. honey ***
pinch of mixed herbs

1   Heat the olive oil in a small saucepan, add the onion and bayleaf, cover, and stew very slowly until soft (about ten minutes). Stir from time to time.
2   Meanwhile, chop the livers roughly, removing any fatty white bits and 'tubes'.
3   Add the tomatoes to the saucepan, break them up roughly with a spoon and bring to the boil.

4 Stir in the livers, herbs and honey. Lower the heat, cover, and simmer very slowly until the livers are no longer pink in the middle, about 12-15 minutes.
5 Discard the bay-leaf and purée the livers.
6 Eat with a little mashed potato for a complete meal.

* Cooked tomatoes can taste very sharp without a little sweetening, but keep the amount very small. We don't normally advise sweetening savoury food.

LIVER, LEEK AND POTATO DINNER

120 g (4 oz) lamb's or chicken liver	2 tsps. of olive oil
75 g (3 oz) white part of a leek	3/4 teacup chicken stock
1 tsp. finely chopped onion	2 tsps. chopped parsley
bay-leaf	2 tsps. cooked potato

1 Clean the leek as described on page 121 and slice thinly.
2 Heat the oil with the bay-leaf in a small saucepan and cook the onion and leek slowly for three minutes.
3 Add the stock, bring to the boil and drop in the livers. Lower the heat to a simmer and cook gently for about eight minutes. From time to time stir and mash lightly with a wooden spoon so the pieces of liver cook evenly.
4 Discard the bay-leaf, add the parsley, and stir for a few seconds. Purée with a little potato.

LIVER, ONIONS AND APPLES

This recipe requires very thin slices of liver. Butchers can supply this with just a little care, but you may have to train your butcher to slice it carefully enough: you're probably the first customer to want it so thin, or to be so precise. Ask for 'paper thin' liver. Say you've had trouble getting liver sliced thinly enough (if you haven't, you will), and ask him how thinly he thinks he can do it. Get him to show you one slice before he does any more. Insist on seeing what he's done before it's wrapped, and reject wedge-shaped slices or any others that are not what you asked for. It's easier to slice evenly from a large piece of liver than from a small bit he's already cut off, so be patient if a small piece is all he has. Be lavish with your praise when he gets it right, so he'll take trouble again next time. Big chunks of liver are offputting to many children, so persevere for the sake of future meals – and stay good-humoured!

Alternatively, use a sharp knife to cut your own thin slices from a tub of chicken livers while they're thawing but still hard.

150 g (5 oz) Cox's apples
120 g (4 oz) onion
120 g (4 oz) thinly sliced liver
1 heaped tsp. of sultanas
1 tsp. of wheatgerm
a little chicken or vegetable stock or water

1   Peel, core and slice the apples. Slice the onions very thinly.
2   Mix the apples, onion and sultanas together and put in layers in the dish with the liver, beginning and ending with the apples and onion.
3   Heat the stock and pour on to barely cover. Sprinkle with wheat-germ.
4   Cook in a covered saucepan at a steady bubble for about 10 minutes.
5   Purée for babies, serve as it is for toddlers.

TURKEY AND CHESTNUTS

Ideal for a baby celebration dinner! It can also be made with chicken and still be special.

120 g (4 oz) cooked turkey meat
50g (2 oz) unsweetened chestnut purée
¹/₂ teacup turkey or chicken stock

Purée together. Leftover chestnut purée can be frozen.

TURKEY AND WINTER VEGETABLES

Again you could substitute chicken.

120 g (4 oz) pieces of cooked turkey meat
240 g (8 oz) mixed vegetables: potato, carrot, parsnip, and
    Brussels sprouts or cabbage
2 cups stock or water

1   Scrub the root vegetables, remove blemishes and slice fairly thinly. Drop into boiling stock and cook until almost done (about 7-10 minutes).

2   Meanwhile, clean the sprouts or cabbage, slice thinly and add to the root vegetables when they are nearly cooked. Bring back to the boil and cook gently for 5-6 minutes. Drain and mash.

3   Boil up the pieces of turkey in the stock for a minute, then purée.

BAMBINO ITALIANO

a puréed meat sauce such as any of the above purées
a little finely grated Edam or Gouda cheese
a little fine pasta

1   Choose very fine or small-shape pasta. Throw it into fast-boiling water and cook at not too fast a boil, uncovered, for 7-10 minutes according to the type of pasta; read the packet for the correct time.

2   Drain, and either use straight away, or save in cold water until needed; the water stops it sticking together in a lump.

3   Purée the sauce with the pasta and warm through. Stir in the grated cheese. As your baby gets older just stir the sauce into the pasta.

> You can cook pasta in advance and keep it in cold water in the fridge for two days. About 30 g (1 oz) of pasta should make up to three baby pasta meals.

FISH TASTERS

Before giving your baby a whole meal of fish, introduce this new flavour by offering tiny tastes when the rest of the family is having a fish meal. Give one flake of fish at a time, sometimes dipped in the tasty sauce that goes with it.

Offer a flake or two of any white fish (whiting, plaice, cod, haddock, etc.):

- with cheese sauce, parsley sauce, mushroom sauce or tomato sauce
- in a little warm milk
- in a little warm milk with a grating of cheese
- with a squeeze of orange juice
- with stewed apricots
- with a few puréed, cooked peas
- with a few cooked mushroom slices
- with a little potato mashed in milk

FIRST FISH DINNER

After you have tried some of the above ideas, choose the ones your baby liked the best and build her first dinner around those flavours. Whiting is a good first fish for a baby to have as it is very easily digested.

Look at the Family Meals section (see page 140) for ideas. Unless you're doing something very simple for your baby, it will probably be easier to cook the fish recipe for everyone in the family. Just omit the salt until you've removed the baby's portion, and check meticulously for bones.

A tiny helping of fish will cook in about one minute in a microwave oven on 'High': simply put the fish on a lightly oiled plate and switch on. Otherwise, put the fish between two plates on top of a pan of boiling water, when it will take up about 10 minutes.

BABY BUBBLE AND SQUEAK

Make this fresh on the day for maximum value.

100 g (4 oz) mashed potato
100 g (4 oz) cooked Brussels sprouts, cabbage, mustard greens
  or broccoli

Mash the greens and mix with the potato. Either serve as it is, or fry in a spot of oil, turning once, until warmed through and with a crispy brown coating.

FRUITY POTATOES

1 small boiled or baked potato
1 tbl. fresh orange juice
1 tbl. full-cream yogurt such as 'Greek'

Skin the potato and simply mash it with the orange juice and yogurt. Don't bother with packet orange juice as the flavour is too weak.

FRESH FRUIT YOGURT

Get your baby used to the taste of yogurt mixed with real fruit, without all the sugar that shop ones have.

'Greek' or other full-cream yogurt
any fresh fruit that will purée
a little fresh orange juice to sweeten

Mix everything together and purée. Sieve also if the fruit had skin or seeds.

COOKED FRUIT YOGURT

fruit and cooking juices as on page 120.
1 tbl. 'Greek' or other full-cream yogurt
mashed ripe banana to sweeten if needed

Stir the fruit and its juice into the yogurt in any proportions and purée as necessary.

Don't think you must add any sugar just because you may be used to very sweet-tasting yogurt. One of the pleasures of yogurt is its clean, tangy flavour: train your baby to enjoy and expect this.

COTTAGE FRUIT

fresh or cooked fruit as above
1 rounded dessertspoon (30 g, 1 oz) cottage cheese
1 tsp. cream cheese (optional)

As above, with the cheese instead of yogurt. The cream cheese adds richness to the purée.

Nine to twelve months: towards family food

Many of the recipes suitable for family meals can be given to babies of this age, although some foods will need mashing. Other foods can now be given in small pieces as finger food.

Finger foods

Babies love eating finger food and it also helps them to learn to bite and chew, long before teeth appear! Make sure that the pieces of food are

- free from peel, pips, stones, small bones, 'strings' and tough membrane
- large enough for inexperienced fingers to hold easily
- large enough for your baby to realise the food must be eaten a little at a time and not swallowed whole
- not too hard

We suggest you try some of the following as finger foods:

- slivers of chicken
- cheese in thin curls, sticks or chunks
- flakes of fish
- pieces of well-cooked meat from a casserole
- pieces of cooked potato, hot or cold
- pieces of bread and toast
- strips of egg white
- pasta shapes
- slices of rolled-up pancakes
- segments of orange, membranes removed
- slices of raw peach, nectarine, kiwi fruit, strawberry, pear, plum, melon, and other smooth textured fruit
- dried apple and pear slices
- dried apricots, cooked for two minutes in hot water
- strips of raw yellow, orange or red peppers – sweeter and more digestible than green
- blanched vegetables – as below:

Brightly coloured vegetables

Vegetables make great finger foods, but some can be very hard to chew. Blanching softens them just that little bit and also turns them a brilliant colour! Try carrot, courgette, parsnip, florets of broccoli and cauliflower, red and yellow peppers, strips of cabbage leaf and halved Brussels sprouts.

Throw the vegetables into fast-boiling water and bring quickly back to the boil. Cook for one minute, uncovered, then drain and put under the cold tap in a sieve. The sudden cold water sets the bright colour.

The nutritional disadvantage of blanching vegetables is that water soluble nutrients (vitamins B and C and all minerals) are partly lost in the blanching water, so save it for cooking vegetables, soups and casseroles. It's got more flavour than plain tap water too!

Dips

Finger foods can be even more attractive if there is something tasty to dip them in and it's so much more fun than eating with a spoon! You could use

- any purée described earlier
- guacamole (recipe on page 135)
- thick yogurt and smatana
- smooth peanut butter (but see page 34)
- tahini or hummus
- cooked sauces such as tomato (recipe on page 156), and milk sauces (page 150) are good with cheese, blanched vegetables and cooked foods such as toast, fish and pasta.

As your baby gets used to the idea of chewing food, rather than just swallowing it, you can offer smaller finger foods such as:

- soft-cooked beans
- cooked or raw fresh peas
- mange tout peas
- mushroom slices
- seedless satsuma and clementine segments
- raisins and sultanas

WHICH BREAD? WHICH CHEESE?

Many kinds! Give a wide variety early on so that the simplest meal of bread and cheese will still be interesting.

Bread

Offer pitta bread, nan, flat Greek loaves, ciabatta, fruit bread, buns, herb bread, rye … whatever you can get, but avoid any containing hard pieces of grain.

Make sure most of the bread you offer is good quality whole-meal: if you rear children on white bread, don't be surprised

---

if they later refuse wholemeal because it needs more chewing. If you have a good baker in your area, you will probably have a range of delicious breads to try out. Many bakers sell day-old bread at half price: a bargain! And try organic bread if you can buy it – or make it.

For a change, warm the bread for a few minutes in the oven, wrapped in foil, to make it taste newly baked. If it's a few days old, sprinkle it with cold water first to rejuvenate it. Sometimes toast it, lightly, perhaps cutting off the crusts first – it depends on the bread you have. Toasting bread or teacakes in front of a fire is a lovely cosy winter treat for anyone!

Cheese

Again, go for variety. Avoid blue cheese at this stage and 'variety' cheeses which may have nuts or other unexpected bits and pieces in, but otherwise give a wide range of different flavours and textures. Don't be afraid of full-flavoured Cheddar cheese: again, if you accustom children to the rubbery 'mild' factory-made sort, don't be surprised if they later reject the real thing, or any other cheese that actually tastes of something. Food is, amongst other things, about flavour. As babies become toddlers, continue to train their tastebuds to expect a variety of tastes in cheese, bread and so on. Children who have been brought up eat a wide range of flavours are less likely to become faddy eaters.

Fresh goats' cheese is an excellent first cheese to give: it is soft and creamy-textured, not very fatty, and doesn't have the lactose content that most cheeses do. Like most good cheese, it's more expensive, but there is so much flavour that a little goes a long way. Most supermarkets have it now.

If you have a specialist cheese shop in your area you are fortunate indeed. Sample some of the wonderful things that never appear in supermarkets. Don't be surprised if your children like flavours that you don't, or if their preferences change.

SOFT GOATS' CHEESE WITH FRUIT

This is an exquisite dish for gourmets of any age! Good as finger food for babies.

tiny slices of 'fresh' (i.e. soft) goats' cheese
thin slices of raw kiwi fruit or other soft-textured fruit*

Make a pattern on your baby's plate with the goats' cheese and fruit.

*Slightly tart fruit is best. Raspberries are excellent, but should be sieved for babies. Try slices of ripe plum, greengage or apricot.

BABY GUACAMOLE

Real guacamole (pronounced gwacka-*mo*-lay) is a Mexican dish, spicy-hot with raw garlic and onion, and eaten with tortilla (corn) chips.

However, if you remove the 'hot' bits and keep the creamy-smooth mild bits, you've got a delicious food for the very young. You can always make a larger amount and add chopped garlic and onion, salt and black pepper for older people to eat with corn chips!

$1/2$ a ripe avocado
1 ripe tomato
dash of olive oil
squeeze of lemon juice

1 First peel the tomato: plunge it hot water for ten seconds, cool under the cold tap and slip off the skin. Cut into quarters, scoop out and discard the seeds. Chop finely.
2 Mash the avocado with the oil and lemon juice until smooth. Stir in the tomato. Use at once before the surface turns brown.

VARIATION: stir in a little smatana or Greek yogurt. Not authentic, but it gives a very pleasant, mild flavour which some babies may prefer.

CHEESE AND POTATO CAKES

This and the next recipe make good dinner dishes with a little salad or green peas. Older children and adults may find them delicious too!

500 g (1 lb) potatoes
50-75 g (2-3 oz) strong Cheddar cheese
2-3 tbl. milk
knob of butter
wholemeal flour for coating
3 drops Worcestershire sauce

1 Scrub the potatoes, boil or steam until soft and slip off the skins. Boil the milk in the same saucepan, then mash the potatoes into the milk with the butter. Beat smooth with a wooden spoon.
2 Grate the cheese and beat in. Shape into 'cakes', any size will do, but make them about 2 cm (½ inch) deep. Coat with flour.
3 Either fry over moderate heat in a little oil for about 5 minutes or until browned on both sides, or bake on a greased tray in a fairly hot oven, turning once, for 15-20 minutes.

PARSLEY FISH CAKES

Not 'fishy' tasting, these can be a good introduction to fish. Add plenty of parsley for a lovely fresh taste.

500 g (1 lb) potatoes
100-150 g (4-5 oz) white fish (whiting, coley, cod, etc.)
2-3 tbl. milk
knob of butter
2 heaped tbl. fresh, chopped parsley
wholemeal flour for coating

1 Scrub the potatoes, boil or steam until soft, then peel.
2 Boil the milk in the same saucepan, then mash the potatoes into the milk with a knob of butter. Beat smooth with a wooden spoon.
3 Meanwhile, cook the fish for 2-3 minutes in the microwave, or steam between two plates over boiling water for about 15 minutes. Skin and flake the fish, remove any bones and mash lightly. Mix with the potato along with the parsley.
4 Shape into 'cakes,' about 2 cm (½ inch) deep and coat with flour.
5 Either fry in oil over moderate-high heat, turning once, until the cakes are browned both sides, or bake on a greased tray in a fairly hot oven, turning once, for 15-20 minutes.

COATING CRUMBS

Pulverised cereal crumbs are excellent for coating as an alternative to flour. All-bran crumbs turn a lovely golden brown colour during frying.

DAIRY DINNER

A creamy-tasting variation on bubble-and-squeak, and a delicious dinner for anyone.

1 medium potato
120g (4 oz) white cabbage
2-3 thin slices of leek
2 tsps olive oil

90 g (3 oz) curd or cream cheese
1 teacup smatana-and-yogurt mixed,
*   OR Greek yogurt*
squeeze of lemon juice
pinch of black pepper

1　Boil the potato, skin and mash. Beat in the cheese and smatana-and-yogurt.
2　Meanwhile, shred the cabbage and leek finely and toss in the oil in a shallow pan over medium heat until cooked, adding a drop of water from time to time to prevent sticking. Mix into the potatoes. Add lemon juice and pepper.
3　Pack into two bowls to make two servings. Good with the following cucumber salad.

BRIGHT GREEN CUCUMBERS

10 cm (2 inches) of cucumber
¹/₂ tsp. lemon juice
¹/₂ tsp. dill weed
tiny pinch black pepper

1　Cut the cucumber into paper thin slices (a food processor or mandolin does this perfectly).
2　Throw into a teacupful of cold water in a small saucepan and bring to the boil. As soon as the cucumber turns bright green, drain and rinse in a sieve under the cold tap to set the colour.
3　Toss the cucumber in the lemon juice diluted with 2 teaspoons of water. Add the dill and a tiny pinch of black pepper.

SPICY SWEDE AND CARROT

carrot
swede
knob of butter
black pepper

1   Take roughly equal quantities of carrot and swede. Peel the swede, scrub the carrot and cut both into chunks.
2   Boil together in vegetable stock or water until soft (about 15 minutes). Drain and mash with a knob of butter and a good pinch of black pepper.
3   Eat with a green vegetable and meat.

FAST FISH

If you have some plain cooked fish ready in the fridge or freezer, this baby meal will be done in no time. Or you could use tinned potatoes and tuna.

50 g (2 oz) cooked cod, separated into flakes
5 cm (1 inch) cucumber, diced or grated
1 tsp. mayonnaise
1 tbl. Greek yogurt or smatana
1-2 baby new potatoes, diced

1   Mix everything together, mashing as necessary and eat!

MIDSUMMER DELIGHT

As good as it sounds. Start it at least half an hour before mealtime and make more so all the family can have some!

3 strawberries
1 tbl. fresh orange juice
$1/2$ tsp. wheatgerm
2 tsps. smatana or Greek yogurt

1   Wash the strawberries: put them in a sieve and hold under the cold tap for a few seconds, then dry by rolling them about on absorbent paper. At the last moment, pull off the green tops.
2   Put the orange juice into a small bowl and slice (or mash) the strawberries into it. Leave for 30 minutes to intensify the flavour of the strawberries – and to flavour the orange juice.
3   Serve with a sprinkling of wheatgerm and a blob of smatana or yogurt which your baby can enjoy stirring in.

BANANA WHIZZ

The drink that's almost a meal! Turn it into a highly nutritious pudding by using it as a sauce over sliced peaches, pears, bananas, apricots or cooked apple.

1 banana, sliced	a grating of nutmeg
4 heaped tbl. plain yogurt	2 drops vanilla extract
2 tbl. fresh orange juice	$^1/_2$ tsp. (or more when you're
1 tbl. milk	used to it) brewers' yeast powder

Whizz everything together in a liquidiser. If you want it thicker make it in advance: it thickens as it stands.

All these recipes make good eating for older children and adults too – just try them out!

BREWERS' YEAST POWDER

An excellent source of iron and B vitamins, brewers' yeast can be added to dishes of many kinds. However, it has a strong flavour so use it in tiny quantities at first. It's available in health food shops.

14

FAMILY MEALS

The following recipes make excellent eating, not just for toddlers, but the whole family. We think they are all delicious and nutritious, and offer a wide range of ingredients and flavours. When cooking for young children just remember:

- don't give nuts, other than finely ground ones, to children under five
- wherever possible, add salt to a dish only after removing the child's portion. (In any case use the bare minimum of salt in cooking. For example, there is no need to add salt when boiling vegetables or pasta.)

Quantities are for two adults unless otherwise stated. You are the best judge of what quantities your children eat.

Breakfast

'Breakfast gets you through the day' is a good motto. Make sure there is time for everyone to have a meal in the morning: boosting blood-sugar levels first thing means less craving for sugary snacks later – and sweeter tempers!

If all else fails, drink a big glass of Banana Whizz (page 139), or Mighty Milk-shake (see page 179). Vary with extra fruit or add powdered milk to make it thicker and creamier-tasting.

PORRIDGE FIT FOR A KING

Forget any ideas you may have about lumpy or otherwise unappetising porridge. This is different. Do use organic oats if you can – the difference in flavour is noticeable.

1 cup organic rolled oats (not jumbo)
2 ¹/₂ cups milk mixed with water
1 small tin evaporated milk
pinch salt
2 tsps. honey, maple syrup OR chopped banana

1 Cook the oats in the milk and water for about 5 minutes over low-medium heat, stirring all the time. Add honey, salt and the evaporated milk, which makes the porridge taste as if you have added cream!
2 But the real secret is to eat it tomorrow, when it will taste even more creamy and delicious. So make up double or treble quantity and have breakfast ready made.

VARIATION: Add a handful of oat- or wheatgerm for extra nutrients or a little oatbran for more fibre. Add a cupful of fresh orange juice at the end for something different.

GREAT GRANOLA

This is the best granola we've tasted yet! It's also a brilliant anytime snack and dessert topping. Omit the nuts for under-fives.

250 g (8 oz) rolled oats
100 g (4 oz) mixed nuts, OR just peanuts
50 g (2 oz) sunflower seeds
50 g (2 oz) sesame seeds
25 g (1 oz) green pumpkin seeds
50 g (2 oz) wheatgerm
3 tbl. sunflower oil
3 tbl. clear honey

1 In a small saucepan heat the oil and honey until pourable.
2 Chop the nuts roughly, mix with all the other dry ingredients, then stir in the oil and honey evenly.
3 Tip into a shallow, oblong baking tray and put into a moderately hot oven for about 20 minutes, turning once or twice. It's done when it's toasted a light golden brown right through.
4 Cool in the tray. When completely cold, store in an airtight container. Enough for a week, though it will keep much longer. Eat with milk, yogurt, fromage frais or fruit juice.

SUPER MUESLI

1 Mix the dry ingredients listed above (without nuts for under-fives). Add flaked wheat and barley if you wish.
2 To serve, add sultanas, banana chips, chopped dates or dried apricots, seedless grapes or banana slices for sweetness, plus some chopped crisp apple. Eat with milk, yogurt, fromage frais or fruit juice.

TINY TODDLERS' BREAKFAST CEREALS

Both Granola and Muesli (above) need a lot of chewing. This is excellent for older children and adults, but not for the very young:

- purée the mixture with milk
- or grind the dry mixture in a food processor
- or grind, then cook in milk to a kind of muesli-porridge

CREAMY SCRAMBLED EGG

10g ($^1/_4$ oz) butter
2 eggs
salt and fresh black pepper
2-3 tsps. water

With a fork, beat the eggs with the water and the seasoning. Cook in the butter in a small pan very, very slowly, stirring all the time, until cooked and creamy. Pile onto hot toast.

VARIATIONS: you can add snipped chives, finely chopped tomato, chopped leftover cooked meat, or grated cheese and so on for variety. One delicious idea is to add finely chopped onion, cooked soft in a drop of oil and water.

Fish

Fish is highly nutritious; aim to eat it often. Here are a few quick, easy and particularly enjoyable recipes.

SCOTTISH HERRING

An exceptionally delicious fish dish that ought to be better known. Herrings are the most nutritious fish available and almost always the cheapest! This old Scottish recipe isn't at all 'fishy' tasting, and it makes a lovely warming winter dinner.

2 herrings
4 tbl. rolled oats
a little sunflower oil for frying
2 tbl. fresh parsley, chopped
1 large lemon
25 g (1 oz) butter

1 Either buy the herrings ready cleaned and filleted, or do it yourself, perhaps as an educational activity with children. This is how:
   a) Wash and gently scrub each herring to remove loose scales
       (you'll have to do this bit anyway) and cut off the fins with scis-
       sors.
   b) With a sharp knife, cut off the head and the tail, plus about
       1 cm (¼ inch) of flesh next to the tail.
   c) Slit open the belly, all the way from the head end to the vent.
       Remove everything inside that will come away and discard
       the whole lot except (if you're lucky) the pale pink roe: save it
       for a tasty snack later (see page 176).
   d) Wash out the inside under the cold tap and shake off the
       water.
   e) Remove the bone – this is fascinating for children to watch!
       To do this, cut down from the vent to the tail, then turn the
       herring onto its stomach on a firm surface. Starting at the
       head end, press gently but quite firmly with your thumbs all
       the way up and down the spine, so the herring opens and flat-
       tens out.
       Keep pressing until you can feel the hard backbone under
       your thumbs. Now press very slightly to the left and to the
       right of the backbone, pushing the flesh off the bone, little by
       little.
       Turn the herring onto its back, hold it down with the fingers
       of one hand while you pull out the backbone with the other
       hand. If it gets stuck somewhere, turn the fish over and press
       a bit more in that spot.
       Most of the 'ribs' will come out attached to the spine, but
       some always get left behind, especially at the head end. You
       must make sure all the large bones are out so be very fussy.
       Ignore, of course, the myriads of tiny, hair-like bones buried
       in the flesh which are soft and completely harmless.
   f) Next, cut down the centre to make two fillets.

g) Feel carefully along both sides of each fillet for hard bony bits that the fins were attached to, and cut these off. The fillets should now be completely bone-free.

2 Have the rolled oats spread out on a piece of clean paper. Lay the fillets on them and press the oats into the fish. Turn the fillets over and coat the second side.

3 Fry very slowly in the oil, skin side first. When golden brown, fry the other side. Allow 7-10 minutes a side, depending on the size of herring.

4 Test whether fish is cooked by pushing the point of a knife into the thickest part of the flesh (see page 145).

5 Put two fillets on each (heated) dinner plate and keep warm.

6 Melt the butter in the pan and immediately add the juice of the lemon, chopped parsley, black pepper and salt. Heat through, then pour over the herrings and eat straight away.

EAT WITH:

- potatoes mashed with hot milk
- a salad of lettuce, spring onion and lots of thin cucumber slices tossed in a drop of olive oil, a good squeeze of lemon, a few grains of caster sugar and fresh black pepper.

VARIATION: For toddlers, mash a few flakes of herring into the potato, along with some of the lovely tangy sauce.

TROUT À LA MEUNIÈRE

This pink-coloured fish makes a wonderful treat. This recipe is virtually the same as the one for Scottish herring, except that flour is used instead of oats. Explain to children that a meunière is a miller's wife, who, presumably, always has plenty of flour!

2 gutted, ready-to-cook, whole rainbow trout (or use trout fillets)	30 g (1 oz) butter 2 tbl. fresh parsley, chopped
2 tbl. wholemeal flour	2 lemons: 1 squeezed, 1 cut into wedges
1-2 tbl. olive oil	salt and fresh black pepper

1 Scale the trout: scrub very well, tail-to-head, with a small stiff brush to remove the mass of tiny grey scales. Cut off the fins with scissors, but (traditionally) leave on the head and 'mitre' the tail fin: cut it into a neat shape with scissors. Wash the trout well and pat dry.

2 Heat the oil in a large shallow pan, coat the trout in flour and fry very slowly for 7-10 minutes or until golden brown underneath. Use a fish slice to turn the trout over very carefully to cook the other side. The trout will probably be done when golden brown both sides, but test as below.

3 Remove to warmed dinner plates. Stir the butter, lemon juice, parsley and seasoning into the pan. Heat and pour at once over the trout.

4 Put two lemon wedges and a chunky parsley sprig on each plate and eat straight away with mashed potato and a tossed green salad as for Scottish herring.

● mind the bones! Remove a few flakes of the pink flesh for children and check for bones. When they're older, they can learn to eat the top fillet, then carefully lift out the spine (and head if it's there) on to a side plate, and then eat the lower fillet.

● crispy treat! Heat a small bowl of plain potato crisps in the oven while you cook the fish and put on the dinner table for everyone to help themselves to a few: they make a good texture contrast to the creamy-smooth fish.

If you're trying to limit such salty snacks, you could treat them as a condiment and occasionally serve small amounts with meals, rather than on their own when they could crowd out more valuable food.

HOW TO COOK DELICIOUS FISH

● fresh fish has virtually no smell: the smell it does have should remind you of the seaside. If it smells 'fishy', it's stale.
● cook the fish S L O W L Y.
● cook as little as possible – until only just done. If you can smell fish cooking, it's being cooked either too long or too fast – or both.
● grilling, baking, steaming, poaching in sauce or good stock, microwaving on a plate or frying in minimum fat are all good methods of preserving flavour. Forget about boiling in tap water if you want fish to be enjoyed. Deep-fried fish adds too much fat to the meal to be recommendable.

- never salt fish before cooking – it will draw out juices that need to be left in. However, marinading is fine, and just a sprinkling of lemon or lime juice half an hour before cooking can enliven indifferent fish.
- when fish is cooked, it will lose its translucence and become opaque right through to the bone. White fish (such as plaice, haddock, cod) become snow white. To test, insert the point of a knife into the thickest part of the fish: the fish is done if you can lift out a flake on the knife. If you cook the fish any more it will go mushy, lose flavour and smell bad.
- sweeten the somewhat dry taste of white fish with peas, parsley, mushrooms, cheese, ratatouille, green beans, onion, milk sauces or tomato sauce.
- serve oily fish (such as herring, mackerel, trout) with tangy fruit such as lemon, lime, gooseberry and apricot.
- have vegetables and salads ready early, so the fish can be eaten as soon as it's done. If you try to keep it warm it will dry out and become overcooked and tasteless. If you find you have a delay, smother the fish in sauce, take it off the heat and reheat quickly at the last moment.
- when you serve fish to children, do check meticulously for bones: just one fright may put them off for life. Some people never eat fish purely because of fear of bones – a great pity, since a bone large enough to be problem is large enough to be seen – and felt with a fork. Teach older children always to check any fish they are given, and if in doubt, to separate each flake.

GRILLED MACKEREL WITH GOOSEBERRY SAUCE

A traditional English dish, well worth reviving. The sweet-sharp sauce is perfect for mackerel.

1 average-sized, very fresh mackerel gutted	15 g ($^1/_2$ oz) butter
	10 g (scant $^1/_2$ oz) flour
450 g (12 oz) green or red gooseberries*, topped and tailed (bottled ones will do though they lack colour)	300 ml. ($^1/_2$ pint) milk
	juice of $^1/_2$ a large lemon
	1 tsp. or so of sugar

*if you can get red gooseberries – and you may have to grow your own – you will have a spectacular crimson sauce that gives this dish tremendous visual appeal.

1   To grill mackerel: Heat the grill while you prepare the mackerel: wash it, cut off the fins with scissors and chop off the tail (and, optionally, the head). Wash and pat dry.
2   Brush the grill rack and the mackerel with olive oil, dust the mackerel in flour, and put it under the hot grill. Immediately lower the heat and cook slowly for about 10 minutes a side until just done.
3   Meanwhile make the sauce: stew the gooseberries in a tablespoon or two of water, stirring until they are soft. Mash lightly. Add the lemon juice and sugar. Set aside.
4   While the gooseberries are stewing, put the butter, flour and milk into a small saucepan and whisk over medium heat to a thickened sauce. Turn the heat very low and stir with a wooden spoon for minute or two longer.
5   Beat the gooseberries into this white sauce, add salt and black pepper; heat and taste: it should be very tangy and slightly sweet.

TO SERVE
One fillet per person, surrounded, not hidden, by plenty of sauce. You need only plainly boiled, jacket or mashed potato to complete the meal. Remove a few fish flakes, sauce and potato for toddlers.

GRILLED MACKEREL WITH APRICOT SAUCE

We wouldn't normally recommend such a sweet sauce, but this one is so scrumptious, and is an exceptionally good way to introduce children to this nutritious fish.

*1 average-sized, very
    fresh mackerel, gutted
1 400 g (14 oz) can of apricots in syrup*
    a small onion, chopped finely
2 tsps. olive oil*

*juice of half a large lemon
1 tsp. ground coriander
a little chopped parsley
    OR fresh coriander
salt and fresh black pepper*

*You could try apricots canned in juice and adding a little sugar, but for some reason this doesn't seem to taste at all as good in this recipe.

1   Grill the mackerel as in the previous recipe.
2   While the fish is cooking, make the sauce as follows:

- Fry the chopped onion in the oil, very slowly until yellow and soft. Add a drop of water from time to time to prevent sticking.
- Drain the apricots and discard virtually all the syrup. Purée the remaining drop with the apricots.
- When the onion is cooked, add the coriander and stir over low heat for a minute. Tip in the apricots, add lemon juice and seasoning and heat through. At the last moment, stir in the parsley and taste: The sauce should be sweet but tangy.

TO SERVE

One fillet per person, surrounded, not hidden, by lots of sauce. Plainly boiled, jacket or mashed potatoes complete the meal. Fat sprigs of parsley look good against the bright yellow sauce. For toddlers, put potato, parsley and flakes of mackerel on a pool of yellow sauce.

HUNGARIAN FISH CASSEROLE

A quick, easy and economical one-pot dish. Enough for four adults.

1 kilo (2 lbs) whiting, cod,
*   haddock or coley, skinned*
25 g (1 oz) butter
2 tbl. olive oil
1 medium onion, sliced
1 clove garlic, chopped
15 g (1/2 oz) cornflour

1 tsp. paprika
1 tbl. tomato purée
250 g (8 oz) tinned tomatoes
*   drained, and juice saved*
1 mug water
bay-leaf
fresh black pepper

1 Cut the fish into chunks and check for bones. Heat the butter and oil in a large saucepan. Fry the onion and garlic over very low heat until soft but not coloured.
2 Dust in the paprika and cornflour. Stir for one minute.
3 Stir in the tomato juice until it bubbles.
4 Lower the heat, stir in the remaining ingredients with pepper to taste. Cover. Simmer for about 5 minutes until the fish is done.

Eat with potatoes and a green vegetable – peas, green beans, broccoli or spinach.

FISH WITH CREAM SAUCE

For a delicious and simple family meal, cook any kind of white fish as below, mask it with cream sauce and eat with plainly boiled potatoes and a sweet green vegetable such as green beans or peas.

The easiest way to cook any white fish is on a lightly oiled, covered plate, either

- in a microwave oven for 3-4 minutes

or

- on top of a saucepan of boiling water for up to 20 minutes.

Few juices are lost and it's easy to catch the exact moment when it is cooked.

CREAMLESS CREAM SAUCE

A smooth, creamy sauce – with no cream!

1 small onion, chopped finely	*15 g ($^3/_4$ oz) flour*
2 tsps. oil	*300 ml ($^1/_2$ pint) milk*
bay-leaf	*1 heaped tbl. or so of powdered milk*
20 g (a good $^3/_4$ oz) butter	*salt and pepper*
OR polyunsaturated margarine	

1 Cook the onion very slowly with the bay-leaf in the oil in a small saucepan for 10 minutes. Add a drop of water if needed to prevent it burning. Discard the bay-leaf.
2 Off the heat, add the fat, flour and all the milk. Whisk over moderate heat until it thickens. Lower the heat and stir for another minute or two to cook the flour well. Stir in the powdered milk to make the sauce taste, amazingly, as if you had added cream! Stir a moment longer and season lightly.

TWO TIPS

- Use a whisk, not a spoon, for a smooth sauce. If any lumps appear, whisk rapidly off the heat until they go.
- You can make this sauce in advance, but cover it with a film of cold milk to stop a skin forming. The sauce will thicken as it cools, but if you whisk in the layer of milk when you reheat it, the finished sauce will be about right.

MUSHROOM SAUCE

cream sauce as above   *speck of butter*
50-100 g (2-4 oz) button mushrooms, *juice of ¹/₂ a small lemon*
   depending on how much   *a grinding of black pepper*
   you like them

1 Wipe the mushrooms with a damp cloth. Don't get them wet or peel them. Slice each one into 3 or 4 and toss over high heat in butter, lemon juice and pepper in a frying pan. They should brown well and smell terrific. They're done when they squeak if pressed with a spoon – a few seconds only (tell children they're done when the mouse squeaks!). Don't let them cook slowly or they'll stew and lose their juice and springiness.
2 Mix into the hot cream sauce, saving a few slices for scattering over the top as garnish. (You could hide a few underneath the fish as surprise treasure!)

PARSLEY SAUCE

cream sauce as above
1-2 tbl. chopped parsley*
¹/₂ teaspoon lemon juice

Mix the parsley and lemon juice into the hot sauce just before serving.

* make sure you use plenty of parsley stalks – that's where most of the flavour and vitamin C is. Chop at the last moment, or much of the flavour and vitamin C will be destroyed by exposure of the cut surfaces to the air.

CHEESE SAUCE

cream sauce as above
40 g (1-2 oz) grated cheese: mature Cheddar, Gouda OR Emmenthal
  are all good
optional dash of Worcestershire sauce and a tiny pinch of cayenne
  pepper or mustard for added flavour

Beat the cheese into the hot sauce little by little so the sauce is glossy.

Pasta

For maximum benefit, use wholewheat pasta as your staple – it looks creamy white when cooked! For a change, sometimes use pasta coloured with spinach or tomato.

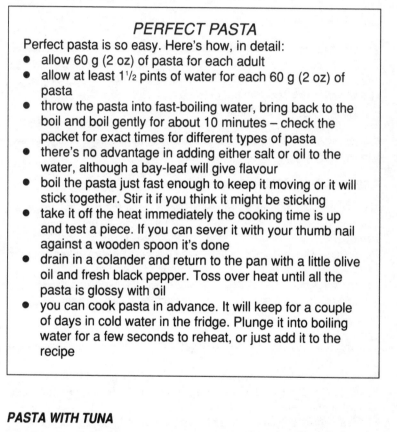

PERFECT PASTA

Perfect pasta is so easy. Here's how, in detail:

- allow 60 g (2 oz) of pasta for each adult
- allow at least 1½ pints of water for each 60 g (2 oz) of pasta
- throw the pasta into fast-boiling water, bring back to the boil and boil gently for about 10 minutes – check the packet for exact times for different types of pasta
- there's no advantage in adding either salt or oil to the water, although a bay-leaf will give flavour
- boil the pasta just fast enough to keep it moving or it will stick together. Stir it if you think it might be sticking
- take it off the heat immediately the cooking time is up and test a piece. If you can sever it with your thumb nail against a wooden spoon it's done
- drain in a colander and return to the pan with a little olive oil and fresh black pepper. Toss over heat until all the pasta is glossy with oil
- you can cook pasta in advance. It will keep for a couple of days in cold water in the fridge. Plunge it into boiling water for a few seconds to reheat, or just add it to the recipe

PASTA WITH TUNA

120 g (4 oz) multicoloured tagliatelle
1 onion, sliced
1-2 cloves garlic, chopped
1 small red pepper, seeded and
  cut into thin strips
1 tbl. olive oil

200 g (6 oz) tin of tuna
1-2 tbl. fresh chopped herbs:
  parsley, chives or basil
dash of tomato purée
fresh black pepper

1 Cook the pasta as on page 151.
2 Meanwhile, stew the onion, garlic and red pepper in the oil until the onion is quite soft and lightly coloured. Add a drop of water occasionally to prevent sticking.
3 Stir in the drained tuna and heat through. Add the cooked pasta, tomato purée, pepper, and, at the last moment, the herbs.

PEASANT PASTA

The easiest pasta dish around – the traditional Italian way, and delicious.

120 g (4 oz) spaghetti or tagliatelle, cooked as above
mixed chopped herbs, fresh or dried
25-50 g (1-2 oz) well-flavoured, grated cheese

Simply stir the herbs and cheese into the pasta. Eat straight away with a green salad.

PASTA WITH BRIGHT RED AND GREEN SAUCE

120 g (4 oz) spaghetti or tagliatelle
1 carrot
1 courgette
1 onion
1 red pepper
1 green pepper
250 g (8 oz) tinned tomatoes
small tin (140 g) tomato purée
good pinch thyme, basil and sage
  (or mixed herbs)
2 pinches of sugar
1 teacup of vegetable stock or water
fresh black pepper
heaped tbl. chopped parsley
Parmesan cheese to serve

1 Chop the onion, slice the courgette, scrub the carrot and slice it very thinly or grate it.
2 Put into a saucepan with the tomatoes, stock, tomato paste, sugar, pepper and mixed herbs. Bring to the boil, then lower the heat, cover, and cook for five minutes.
3 Meanwhile, boil some water for the pasta and slice the peppers.
4 Stir the peppers into the other vegetables and cook steadily for ten minutes stirring from time to time.
5 As soon as you have started cooking the peppers, throw the pasta into the boiling water, return the water to the boil, then cook at moderate speed for ten minutes or until you can sever the pasta with your thumb nail.

6 Drain the pasta and stir immediately into the bright red and green sauce. Stir in half the chopped parsley and serve with the remaining parsley scattered on top.

7 Eat with grated cheese.

SPAGHETTI BOLOGNESE

Iron-rich liver will benefit the entire family. It's well-disguised here in this fabulous sauce. Enough for two hearty adult appetites.

120 g (4 oz) wholewheat spaghetti
1 carton (227 g, 8 oz) frozen
  chicken livers, thawed
1 large onion, chopped
2 cloves garlic, chopped
2 tbl. olive oil
2 tsps. wholewheat flour

50-100 g (2-4 oz) mushrooms,
  wiped, sliced
1-2 tsps. tomato ketchup
pinch basil, thyme and sage
fresh black pepper
600 ml (1 pint) stock or water
grated Gouda, Edam or
  Parmesan to serve

1 Heat the oil in a medium saucepan and soften the onion in it for 10 minutes over a gentle heat, stirring from time to time to prevent sticking. Allow to colour slightly; add the garlic half way through.

2 Add the livers and stir for a minute. Dust in the flour and stir for a further minute. Pour in all the stock along with the other ingredients, stir and bring to the boil.

3 Lower the heat and simmer slowly, uncovered, to a good, thickened sauce – about half an hour, stirring occasionally.

4 Meanwhile cook the pasta as on page 151. Serve the sauce on top of a pile of pasta and with a tossed green salad.

VARIATION: add chopped ham to the sauce at the end of the cooking time.

—— Meat and vegetarian dishes ——

WOLF STEW

This is another way of giving the family nutrient-rich liver without even mentioning the word! This recipe has pieces of liver in a mouthwatering sauce. Perhaps your children will try to guess which part of the wolf they're eating!

250 g (8 oz) lambs OR	*1 heaped tbl. wholewheat flour*
pigs liver, sliced thinly	*1 heaped tsp. paprika*
1 medium-sized onion, chopped	*150 ml ($^1/_4$ pint) chicken stock*
2-3 cloves garlic, chopped	*250 g (8 oz) tin of tomatoes*
2 tbl. oil	*pinch of thyme, sage*
1 red pepper, sliced	*and black pepper*
25 g (1 oz) sunflower margarine	
OR butter	

1 Heat the oil and half the butter in a fairly large saucepan. Toss the liver in it over a low heat for one minute, then lift out onto a plate and set aside.

2 Put the onion and garlic into the saucepan, stir round, cover and cook slowly for five minutes. Add the red pepper, replace the lid and cook for another five minutes, shaking the pan and stirring now and again to prevent sticking.

3 Meanwhile, use scissors to cut the liver into even-sized but irregular shapes.

4 Melt the remaining butter in the pan. Dust in the flour and paprika, raise the heat a little and stir for five minutes to cook and lightly brown the flour. Scrape the bottom of the pan well as you stir.

5 Tip in the tomatoes and stock. Stir and bring to the boil. Simmer, until the sauce begins to thicken – about two minutes.

6 Add the liver and herbs, and cook gently for about two more minutes until the liver is done, stirring frequently. Never overcook liver or it will go hard and dry. It's ready when it has just stopped being pink in the middle. You could snip a piece in half with scissors to inspect it.

7 Serve with jacket or boiled potatoes cut into chunks.

*VARIATION: Add green, orange or yellow peppers, broccoli or cauliflower pieces, diced carrot, courgette or parsnip, sweetcorn or whatever you think your family might find amusing in a wolf stew!

Kidney, cut into thin slices, could be used sometimes instead of liver.

PIZZA

A good home-made pizza is a real treat. This is easily the best we know.

Base

125 g (4 ¹/₂ oz) plain flour, half wholemeal, half white
60 ml (2 fl oz) milk
60 ml (2 fl oz) olive / sunflower oil
15 g (¹/₂ oz) fresh yeast or 10 g (¹/₄ oz) dried
tomato sauce (see page 156)

Topping

1 ball Mozzarella* or 5 oz Gouda
30-50 g (1-2 oz) grated Parmesan
any combination of the following: sliced mushrooms, stoned black olives, shredded ham, flaked sardines, pilchards or tuna, sliced Italian salami, tiny blanched broccoli florets, little heaps of cooked, well-drained spinach, etc.

Use a circular pizza tray or shallow baking tray about 25 by 35 cm (10 by 14 inches)

1 First make the dough
   - Crumble the yeast into a small bowl and add the milk, heated to tepid. Stir and leave to dissolve in a warm place for about 10 minutes. Add the oil.
   - Mix in the flour and knead with your hands a make a very soft, pliable dough. If it seems at all dry, then add milk or water immediately. Knead for about 3 minutes to make the dough elastic.
   - Put it into a greased bowl and wrap the bowl in a plastic bag. Leave it in a warm place (a sunny windowsill will do) to rise to twice its size – about half an hour.
2 Meanwhile make the sauce and prepare the toppings. Lightly grease the pizza tray.
3 Heat the oven to gas 8, 450°F, 225°C. Have a shelf positioned fairly near the top of the oven. (If your circular pizza tray bumps into the back of your oven shelf, raise the tray by standing it on an up-turned quiche tin.)
4 Roll the dough out thinly on a floured surface. Use the rolling pin to lift it onto the pizza tray and pinch it up all the way round to make a little wall.
5 Cover with an even layer of tomato sauce, scatter slices of Mozzarella (or grated Gouda) over it and then add your toppings, ending with the Parmesan.

6 Bake for exactly 10 minutes. Wait a few minutes before slicing to allow the cheese to set. Eat with a big green salad.

*Mozzarella can also be bought in blocks, but these are larger than the original Italian ball shapes – and more expensive.

GREEN SALAD FOR PIZZA – OR ANYTHING

several different kinds of lettuce, e.g.   *sprigs of watercress*
    cos, round, Webb's, curly endive   *mustard and cress*
diced cucumber   *pieces of baby spinach leaves*
thinly sliced spring onion   *tiny sticks of raw*
    OR mild white onion   *Brussels sprouts*

Wash and dry the leaves, and put everything into a large salad bowl. At the last moment, toss with a teaspoon or so of olive to make it shine, then toss in Family Salad Dressing (see next recipe).

FAMILY SALAD DRESSING

The sugar in this dressing brings out the fruitiness of the olive oil and stops it tasting too oily. You can make up the dressing in advance and store in a stoppered jar in the fridge. Shaking the jar just before using is an easy and very good way of mixing the ingredients. Children could be involved in the preparation of easy salads – as well as shaking the jar of dressing!

1-2 tbl. olive oil   *tiny pinch salt*
1 tsp. lemon juice   *2-3 grindings fresh black pepper*
2-3 drops wine / cider vinegar   *optional: 1-2 cloves garlic,*
tiny pinch sugar   *crushed to a paste*

Mix all together. Add to salads just before eating or they will wilt.

ITALIAN TOMATO SAUCE

An excellent and immensely useful sauce. Use it on fish or chicken with rice and spinach, in lasagne, on pizza, with beans, on spaghetti, or in almost any recipe that calls for tomato sauce. Perhaps make up a large quantitiy and freeze in small containers.

1 large onion, chopped	*2 tsps. tomato ketchup*
bay-leaf	*good pinch of thyme, sage, basil*
2 tbl. olive oil	*pinch of black pepper and salt*
2 cloves garlic, chopped	*tiny pinch cayenne*
1 kilo (2 lbs) tinned tomatoes	

1 Cook the onion and garlic in the oil for 7-10 minutes to soften and lightly colour. Add everything else.
2 Bring to the boil. Lower the heat and cook uncovered over moderate heat, stirring occasionally, to a thickened sauce, about 30 minutes. Taste for seasoning.

TOMATO PIE

Very similar to the pizza recipe, but quicker, as there is no dough to rise.

Pastry	**Filling**
150 g (6 oz) flour	*tomato sauce as above: half quantity*
100 g (4 oz) butter	*50 g (2 oz) grated Cheddar cheese*
6 tsps. ice water	*a few sliced mushrooms*
	6-8 pitted black olives

a 20 cm (7-8 inch) pie tin

1 Make up the pastry and chill while you make the sauce (there are detailed pastry-making instructions on page 78).
2 Heat the oven to gas 6-7, 415°F, 205°C. Put a solid shelf in the oven just above half way up.
3 Roll out the pastry to line the tin. There should be some left over to freeze for another time. Prick the base all over well with a fork. Line the pastry with two layers of tissue paper, fill with dried beans or peas and bake blind on the solid shelf for 10 minutes. Remove the beans and paper and cook another 10 minutes.
4 Pour in the tomato sauce, scatter on the mushrooms, the olives and then the cheese. Replace in the oven to melt the cheese slightly – or grill for a few seconds, but take care the pastry rim doesn't burn.

Eat while hot with plainly boiled potatoes and a good green salad.

HURRY CURRY

A very mild curry, more aromatic than spicy, sweet with fruit, and quite suitable for toddlers. Quick to prepare.

1 medium-sized onion, sliced	*2 chicken breasts*
1 clove garlic, chopped	*squeeze of lemon juice*
1 tbl. sunflower oil	*150 ml ($^1/_4$) pint chicken stock*
15 g ($^1/_2$ oz) butter	*$^1/_2$ tin mango slices (OR peach,*
$^1/_2$ tsp. curry paste (OR powder)	*pineapple or plum)*
$^1/_2$ tsp. turmeric	*a little yogurt to serve*

1 Heat the oil and butter in a shallow pan and cook the onion in it for five minutes over a low heat, then add the garlic and continue cooking for four minutes, stirring occasionally. Meanwhile, cut the chicken into strips the size of your little finger.
2 Add the curry paste and turmeric to the onion, and stir for one minute to mellow the spiciness. Add the chicken pieces, then tip in the stock and lemon juice, stir smooth and bring to the boil.
3 Lower the heat and half cover. Simmer gently for about 10 minutes or until the chicken is cooked through, stirring from time to time.
4 Drain the mango and cut each slice into three, lengthways. Heat gently in its juice in a small saucepan.
5 When the chicken is done, dish onto dinner plates, swirl in the yoghurt, and garnish with the heated mango slices. Discard the highly sweetened syrup. Eat straight away with rice – and poppodums for fun.

AND THE LEFTOVER MANGO SLICES?
You could purée the left-over mango slices with orange juice and yogurt for a delicious fruity drink or simply add them to the Mighty Milkshake on page 179.

HOW TO COOK BROWN RICE

Get children used to brown rice from an early age; if you postpone it they'll complain about its non-pure-white colour and the extra chewing. White rice is more calorie-dense and you may prefer this for babies, but after that go for brown: it's higher in B vitamins, iron, calcium and potassium and has valuable fibre.

1 teacup brown rice (about 120 g, 4 oz)
2 ¹/₂ teacups water

1   Wash the rice in a sieve under the cold tap, drain well by shaking
    the sieve and then standing it on a thickly-folded dishcloth.
2   Boil the water in a small, heavy saucepan with a well-fitting lid.
3   Throw the rice into the water, bring quickly back to the boil and
    skim with a large spoon.
4   Turn the heat down to the lowest possible, cover tightly, and cook:

● long grain rice needs 30 minutes
● short/round grain rice needs 25 minutes.
● narrow grain (such as Basmati) rice needs 15-20 minutes

Don't stir rice while it's cooking.

At the end of the cooking time, the rice should have absorbed the
water and be perfectly cooked. Don't try to rinse it – or you'll simply
be rinsing away all the water soluble nutrients!

Eat it straightaway, or keep it warm for a few minutes on a plate in a
low oven.

GOLDEN RICE FOR CURRIES

Fry a little chopped onion in oil until soft, add a teaspoonful of
turmeric and stir over heat for one minute. Add a teacupful or so of
cooked rice and stir in to colour.

VARIATION: add a spoonful of cooked peas at the last moment, or a few
roasted peanuts as an added treat.

GOLDEN SESAME SLICES

An invaluable and delicious vegetarian dish. Freeze portions of it so
you've always got a vegetarian option available. This quantity makes
six adult servings.

550 g (1 lb 2 oz) carrots   *25-50 g (1-2 oz) sesame seeds*
250 g (8 oz) grated Cheddar cheese *50 ml (2 fl oz) milk*
75 g (3 oz) rolled oats   *50 g (2 oz) butter, melted*
1 rounded tbl. wholewheat flour   *pinch salt and fresh black pepper*

a greased, shallow baking tin about 30 by 22 cm (8 by 12 inches)

1 In a large bowl mix the oats, flour, salt, pepper, the grated cheese and half the sesame seeds.
2 Scrub the carrots, grate them and stir in.
3 Pour the milk onto the melted butter and stir in.
4 Press into the prepared tin; sprinkle with the remaining seeds. Bake at gas 5, 375°F, 190°C for 25 minutes or until golden brown.

Cut into slices and eat with mashed potatoes and a cooked green leafy vegetable – or with bubble and squeak.

BABY MEATBALLS WITH DILL

250 g (8 oz) minced beef
1 tbl sunflower oil
15 g (¹/₂ oz) butter
300 ml (¹/₂ pint) Greek yogurt
1 tsp. dill weed
pinch salt and fresh black pepper

1 Mix the beef with a pinch of the dill, salt, pepper and a teaspoon of the yogurt. Shape into 12 tiny meatballs. If you have time, chill them for half an hour so they'll hold together well when you cook them.
2 Heat the oil in a shallow pan. Roll the meatballs about in the pan until well-browned on the outside and cooked through. Turn the heat low after the first minute or two or the outside will char. Put onto warmed serving plates.
3 Off the heat, add the butter to the hot pan and allow to melt. Then, over a very low heat stir in the remaining dill and yogurt. Don't overheat or the yogurt will curdle; if it does, ignore it – it will taste the same!
4 Season with pepper and pour over the meatballs. Eat at once with jacket or mashed potato and a crisp green salad.

VARIATION: make this mixture into burger shapes if you think that would be more popular, in which case don't forget to call them burgers!

HOME-MADE BURGERS

Nothing wrong with a good home-made burger from time to time. Just:

- choose lean meat. Allow 75-100 g (3-4 oz) per adult
- put in plenty of onion and garlic, chopped very finely (or it will pop out)
- season with herbs and spices rather than salt. Try thyme, sage and marjoram; add a spot of ketchup, which will help to hold the burger together, and specks of mustard or cayenne.
- be crafty – without telling anyone, mix in small amounts of more nutritious meats, finely chopped, such as liver or heart
- try adding finely grated carrot – carrot and beef are natural allies
- grill rather than fry
- serve with plenty of salad and a big jacket potato as a main meal, or in a salad-filled wholemeal bap.
- instead of sugary relishes and so on, toss the salad in a quick olive oil dressing (see recipe on page 156)

VARIATION: also, try vegetarian burgers: the next recipe is delicious.

BEANBURGERS

There are lots of variations on this theme, but this is a good basic recipe. As it takes a little time to prepare, make a big batch and freeze.

250 g (8 oz) red lentils
900 ml (1 1/2 pints) boiling water
about 500g (1 lb) finely chopped
vegetables, such as onion, carrot,
  garlic, celery, celeriac,
  red pepper, broccoli

1/2 tsp. cayenne pepper
pinch salt and fresh black pepper
2 tbl. tomato purée OR ketchup
1/2 tsp. dry mustard
wholemeal flour for coating

1 First cook the lentils to a soft mass that will just hold its shape:
  - Pick over the lentils, then throw into a large saucepan of fast boiling water. Boil fast, uncovered, for 10 minutes.
  - Lower the heat, and, stirring often, cook for another 15-20 minutes until completely soft. The mixture will stiffen as it cools.
2 Meanwhile, either steam or stir-fry the vegetables.
3 When the lentils have cooled, beat in the tomato purée and seasonings, then carefully fold in the cooked vegetables.
4 Shape into burgers. Coat in wholewheat flour or crushed cereal and fry in very little oil until golden, turning once. Alternatively, bake on a greased tray in a hot oven, gas 7-8, 440°F, 230°C, for about ten minutes, turning once.

VARIATION: try topping with a mixture of grated cheese and whole-wheat breadcrumbs and grilling to melt the cheese.

Eat with jacket potatoes or oven chips and either a big mixed salad or cooked green vegetables.

CHICKEN PIE

Always a popular dish. Almost any proportion of chicken, ham and mushrooms will do and you can omit the ham and mushrooms and still have a good dish. The total amount depends on the size of your pie dish. For the amounts given here, a 600 ml (one pint) capacity dish is about right.

*500g (1 lb) cooked chicken meat
  cut into slivers*
*100 g (4 oz) mushrooms,
  sliced thickly*
50 g (2 oz) cooked ham, chopped
*2 teacups chicken stock
  (approximately)*

*3 heaped tsps. wholewheat flour
knob of butter OR
  polyunsaturated margarine
pinch thyme
1 tbl. chopped parsley
100g (4 oz) pastry (see page 78)*

1 Before you start, check that the chicken, ham and mushrooms together come up to the top of your pie dish, or the crust will fall in!
2 Toss the chicken, mushrooms and ham together with the herbs and a little seasoning, and fill your pie dish.
3 Mix the flour into a little of the stock. Heat the rest of the stock with the butter in a small saucepan, then stir into the flour mixture. Pour back into the saucepan, stir until thickened, then pour into the pie dish. It should come about three-quarters of the way up.
4 Roll out the pastry and cut a strip to fit the rim. Wet the rim with water or stock and stick on the pastry strip. Wet the strip. Cover with the rest of the pastry and seal the edges. Make a hole in the middle for steam to escape. Decorate*, if you have time, with pastry leaves – a nice job for a child! Brush with milk, sprinkle very lightly with salt and pepper, and bake at once at gas 6 ½, 415°F, 220°C, about 20 minutes or until golden brown.

Serve with potatoes, carrots or parsnips and a green leafy vegetable.

*If you decorate the pie with pastry leaves, have these ready cut beforehand so they can be put in place quickly. If you wait too long, the steam from the heated stock will begin to melt the pastry crust.

Desserts

FRESH FRUIT

The best desserts for children of any age are those based on fruit. Of course milk puddings can be a good way of giving milk to a child who won't drink milk, and there's something to be said for occasionally cooking traditional puddings, perhaps as a Sunday wintertime treat, so that children learn what these delicious dishes are. But for every day, stick to fruit.

It doesn't have to be made into a 'pudding'. You could simply wash some fruit and put out in such ways as:

- a fruit pyramid! Build a pyramid of (washed) satsumas, or of clementines, baby Cox's apples, plums, etc.
- a bowl of whole (washed) mixed fruits, to be cut up at the table
- one peach or nectarine on each person's plate with a small knife
- a serving platter of several fruits in small amounts: bunchlets of 3-4 grapes, bananas cut diagonally into thirds (they don't have to be peeled), melon or pineapple wedges, orange or ugli-fruit segments, a few plums, greengages, golden gooseberries, cherries, apricots ... whatever's in season
- a slice of melon for each person. Salt, surprisingly, brings out the flavour! Try wedges of watermelon in hot weather
- fresh pineapple: cut off the leaf end with a small slice of fruit attached, and stand it in the middle of a large plate. Peel the rest of the pineapple, slice, core, and overlap the slices in a circle around the leaves. Spectacular looking, and good enough for a dinner party

WINTER FRUIT SALAD

This can be made in ten minutes. It's tangy with grapefruit, sweet with orange, crisp with apple and creamy-sweet with banana.

1 small, red-skinned Cox's apple
1 orange
1 grapefruit
1 banana

Wash the apple put don't peel. Chop all the fruit and mix together. If you make it in advance, save the banana for adding at the last moment.

VARIATION: top with granola, see page 141.

HOW TO PREPARE CITRUS FRUIT

- With a sharp knife, cut a slice off the 'north and south pole' ends of the fruit, exposing the flesh.
- Stand the fruit on one of the cut ends and cut off the peel in strips. Make sure you take off all the pith as you go.
- The really correct thing to do next is to cut either side of each membrane so each segment drops out, succulent and membrane free. Delectable, but time consuming for every day.
- An alternative, very quick way, is to hold the fruit on its 'side,' and slice into rounds. Then cut these (you can cut two or three at a time) into six or eight wedges. Save the juice and add to the dish.

CREAMY WINTER FRUIT

Another quickie. Utterly delicious. You can add a dash of Cointreau or Grand Marnier and use it as a dinner party dish! Make sure the fruit is fully ripe.

1 Comice pear
1 large banana
1 teacupful fresh tangerine or orange juice
1 teacupful smatana OR Greek yogurt
a grating of nutmeg
2-3 drops vanilla extract

1   Mix the smatana, juice, nutmeg and vanilla.
2   Cut the fruit into chunks and stir in.

LAST MINUTE BANANA YOGURT DESSERT

1 large banana, sliced
approximately 2 teacups of thick yogurt
a squeeze of lemon juice
2 tsps. honey
2 tsps. wheatgerm or granola

In each dessert bowl mix 1 teaspoon of honey and 1 teaspoon of wheatgerm with a little lemon juice. Toss the banana slices in this mixture, then top with yogurt. Serve nice and cold.

HOW TO WASH STRAWBERRIES

Wash them quickly under the cold tap in a sieve, then dry by rolling them about on several thicknesses of kitchen paper. Pull off the green tops at the last moment.
This method leaves them looking clean and shiny and with-out a 'washed' look.

STRAWBERRY-RASPBERRY DESSERT

a dozen or so large strawberries
1 1/2 teacups fresh orange juice
2 teacups thick yogurt or smatana
1 teacupful or more of raspberries
1 tsp. sieved icing sugar

1 Slice the strawberries into fresh orange juice in each dessert bowl.
2 Sieve the raspberries, beat in the icing sugar and mix into the yogurt. Mask the strawberries with this.

If you have time, leave the strawberries marinading in the juice for a while before mealtime to enhance their flavour.

FRESH FRUIT COMPOTE

Use soft-textured fruits only for this. A preponderance of red fruit looks particularly good. Choose from:

strawberries, raspberries, loganberries, cherries, black, red and white currants, melon, bananas, mango, papaya, passion fruit, pears, peaches, nectarines.

Cut up the large fruit and mix all together in a bowl with very little fresh orange juice. Leave at least an hour to marinate. You could warm it very gently in the oven or microwave, just long enough to make the juices run. Don't overdo it or you'll just have stewed fruit.

FRESH FRUIT JELLY: TERRINE DES FRUITS

A spectacular party dish for any age group. Use any soft-textured fruit in season except fresh pineapple, which contains an enzyme that will stop the gelatine setting.

FOR SIX ADULT HELPINGS:

3 kiwi fruit, peeled, sliced thinly *a few red currants or raspberries*
3 bananas, sliced into three, lengthways *3 oranges, segmented*
1 box strawberries *300 ml (¹/₂ pint) orange juice*
¹/₂ a pink melon, thinly sliced *20 g (³/₄ oz) powdered gelatine*

1 Heat half the orange juice in a small saucepan. Off the heat, sprinkle on the gelatine and whisk to dissolve. If any undissolved grains remain, reheat very gently without letting it boil, and whisk again. Pour in the rest of the juice and set aside.
2 Wash the strawberries as on page 165. Slice each berry into three.
3 Lightly but thoroughly oil a large loaf tin. Put the fruit into the tin in neat layers, beginning with the kiwi fruit. Scatter red currants or raspberries here and there as you go.
4 When you've used up all the fruit pour in the orange juice mixture. Put in the fridge to set.
5 To turn out: slide a blunt knife round the sides of the tin and wipe the base with a dishcloth wrung out in hot water. Tip out on to a wet serving plate and slide it, if necessary, into position.
6 Surround with sprays of lemon balm or puréed mango and serve with thick yogurt.

FRESH FRUIT TRIFLE

¹/₂ packet trifle sponges
fresh fruit jelly, as above, using any fruit except fresh pineapple

450 ml ($^3/_4$ pint) Greek yogurt
150 ml ($^1/_4$ pint) thick cream
a little extra fruit for decoration

1   Slice the sponges in half lengthways, place on the bottom of a large trifle bowl and cover with the fresh fruit and jelly mixture. Let set.
2   When quite set, whisk the cream to just thickened, mix it into the yogurt and spread over the top of the jelly.
3   Decorate with fresh fruit at the last moment so the fruit juices don't stain the yogurt mixture and make it look tired.

STRAWBERRY JELLY RING

A variation on the Terrine des Fruits recipe opposite.

FOR SIX ADULT HELPINGS:

2 boxes of strawberries
300 ml ($^1/_2$ pint) orange juice
20 g ($^1/_2$ oz) gelatine

a $1^1/_2$ pint capacity (19 cm diameter) ring mould

1   Prepare the strawberries as on page 165. Slice each berry into three.
2   Heat half the orange juice in a small pan. Off the heat, sprinkle on the gelatine evenly and whisk to dissolve. If, after two or three minutes, the gelatine hasn't completely dissolved, heat gently and whisk again.
3   Whisk in the remaining juice.
4   Lightly but thoroughly oil the mould, put a neat layer of strawberry slices on the bottom and round the outer edge, then pile the rest in the middle.
5   Pour in the juice gently (the strawberries will tend to float around a bit) and leave to set in the fridge.
6   To turn out: slide a flexible blunt knife round the outer and inner edges, then wipe the base with a dish cloth wrung out in hot water. Tip out onto a wet plate and slide into the centre.

ICE-CREAM PUDDING WITH MERINGUES

Not real ice-cream, but it tastes very similar when eaten very cold. It's an old wartime recipe, very economical and nutritious. The sugar has been cut by half in this version.

FOR FOUR ADULT HELPINGS:

Ice cream
25 g (1 oz) sugar
50 g (2 oz) butter
40 g (1 ¹/₂ oz) white flour
1 egg yolk pinch of salt
2 drops vanilla extract
600 ml (1 pint) milk

Meringue
1 egg white
1 heaped tbl. caster sugar
tiny pinch salt

To make the ice cream
1 Heat the milk in a medium-sized saucepan to fairly hot and set aside.
2 Cream the butter and sugar until pale and fluffy. Beat in the egg yolk with half the flour.
3 Whisk 2 tablespoons of the hot milk into the butter mixture and when smooth, whisk in the rest of the flour.
4 Whisk in the rest of the milk, a little at a time, whisking smooth between each addition. Pour into the saucepan and stir over a low heat to a thickened custard. Don't let it boil or it could curdle. When one bubble breaks on the surface, it's done. Stir in the salt and vanilla.
5 Pour at once into a serving dish and cover closely with greaseproof paper to prevent a skin forming. Cool, then chill in the fridge. Serve cold as ice-cream with fruit, or as a pudding with the meringue.

To make the meringue
1 Whisk the egg white to just stiff in a good-sized bowl. Stop whisking immediately your whisk can pick up a 'snowball' of meringue that doesn't droop. Whisk in half the sugar with a pinch of salt, then gently stir in the rest.
2 Straightaway, use a teaspoon to put blobs of meringue on a lightly greased baking sheet. Cook until completely dry at your oven's lowest setting, possibly for an hour – it depends on your oven.

3 Cool on a wire tray. It doesn't matter if some crumble! When they are completely cold, they will keep very well in the fridge or freezer in an air-tight container. Scatter them on top of the pudding at the last moment so they don't go soft.

VARIATION: scatter brightly coloured fruit among the meringues; raspberries look terrific.

APRICOT JELLY CRUNCH

Very popular as a family pudding or party dish.

FOR FOUR ADULT HELPINGS:

250 g (8 oz) dried apricots	*1 sachet gelatine (12g, ¹/₂ oz)*
2 strips of orange rind	*¹/₄ tsp. mixed spice*
1 strip of lemon rind	*1 tsp. clear honey*
a small squeeze of lemon juice	*300 ml (¹/₂ pint) smatana*
2 teacups fresh orange juice	*OR Greek yogurt*
	a handful of granola, (see page 141)

If you don't have any granola, just omit it – the pudding will still be delicious.

1 Put the apricots in a sieve and pour boiling water over them to clean them. Then put them into a small bowl, cover them with two teacups of cold water and drop in the orange and lemon peel. Leave to soak a few hours or overnight.
2 Bring the apricots and their soaking water to the boil, cover and simmer slowly about 40 minutes or until soft. Discard the peel.
3 Boil a teacupful of fresh orange juice in a small saucepan. Remove from the heat, sprinkle on the gelatine and whisk to dissolve. If any grains remain undissolved, gently reheat without boiling, and whisk again. Allow two or three minutes for the gelatine to dissolve completely, then whisk in the honey, lemon juice and the second teacup of (cold) orange juice.
4 Liquidise or sieve the apricots and their juice. Stir in the spice, and the gelatine mixture. Pour into a serving bowl and put in the fridge to set.
5 Cover with a layer of yogurt or smatana; just before serving top with granola.

RASPBERRY CRUNCH

Greek yogurt
roughly crushed ginger biscuits (or mixed ginger and digestives)
lots of raspberries, fresh or frozen

Fill individual goblets with the three ingredients, beginning and ending with the yogurt. At the last moment, top with a large raspberry.

GRANDMOTHER RACHEL'S POLISH CHEESECAKE

A very good special occasion cheesecake which is easy to make.

FOR SIX ADULT HELPINGS:

200 g (8 oz) crushed digestive biscuits *35 g (1 ¹/₂ oz) butter*
75 g (3 oz) melted butter OR margarine *25-50 g (1-2 oz) sugar*
500 g (1 lb) curd cheese *tiny pinch cinnamon and salt*
150 ml (¹/₄ pint) smatana *3 eggs, separated*
  OR thick yogurt *grated rind and juice*
handful sultanas *1 lemon*

a 25 cm (9-10 inch) diameter quiche or gratin dish.

1 Pour boiling water over the sultanas and leave to plump up.
2 Line your dish with the biscuits mixed with the 75g (3 oz) butter. Bake at gas 7, 425°F, 210°C for three or four minutes.
3 Meanwhile cream the 35 g (1½ oz) butter with the sugar until pale and fluffy. Beat in the three egg yolks one by one and then add the cheese and the smatana.
4 Beat in the soaked sultanas, lemon juice and rind, salt and cinnamon.
5 Whisk the egg whites until stiff and fold in. Fill the crumb crust.
6 Bake at gas 7, 375°F, 185°C for about ten minutes. Eat cold, on its own or with fresh raspberries, blueberries or loganberries.

15
SNACKS

Always have something around for hungry children to nibble on when they cannot wait for the next meal! Have fresh or dried fruit, raw vegetable sticks and milk available for quick nibbles, but for something more substantial try some of the following.

Breadmaking

The best snack in the world is good bread. Here's a particularly delicious recipe, plus a few hints for beginners. Try a breadmaking session with children when you've mastered the technique – or learn together.

BREADMAKING TIPS
- the better the flour the better the bread. If you can, buy flour from a named mill (usually from a grocer or wholefood shop), rather than an ordinary supermarket blend. It makes a difference.
- Buy 'strong' (durum) flour for bread; the grains of wheat it's ground from are harder and will help the bread to rise.
- Buy fresh yeast if you possibly can from a baker's shop. You can buy it a little at a time or in a block weighing over two pounds. Chop up the block, reassemble and freeze for up to three months.

- Never buy dried yeast in a tin – once opened it deterio-rates. Buy individual sachets.
- The commonest fault in bread-making is adding too little water, resulting in a tough, dry dough that won't rise and which produces bricks instead of bread. Keep the dough on the wet side right from the beginning: you can easily add more flour, but it's very hard to incorporate extra water into a dry dough.
- Cook the bread thoroughly. Underdone bread is inedible. If in doubt give it another five minutes.
- Never wash bread tins! They will get thoroughly sterilised every time you bake, and gradually they will develop their own non-stick coating. If you keep washing this off you could have trouble getting the loaves out.

TO MAKE ONE LARGE LOAF:

500 g (generous 1 lb) plain flour, about $^2/_3$ wholemeal, $^1/_3$ unbleached white
25 g (1 oz) fresh yeast or 15 g ($^1/_2$ oz) dried
1 tsp. salt
1-2 tsp. black treacle or molasses
180 ml (6 fl oz) hot water
180-280 ml (6-9 fl oz) cold water – or more

a well-oiled large loaf tin: 19 cm by 12 cm by 9 cm deep (7 $^1/_2$" by 4 $^1/_2$" by 3 $^1/_2$") is about the right size

1   Pour the hot water onto the molasses in a jug and stir to dissolve. Add the same amount of cold water to make the water cool enough not to kill the yeast.
2   Drop in the yeast, cover, and leave for about 15 minutes in a warm place to bubble. Meanwhile mix the flours and salt in a large mixing bowl. Make a 'well' in the flour.
3   Add the remaining cold water to the yeast and tip into the well in the flour.
4   Mix up, first with a wooden spoon and then with your hands to make a soft, moist dough. If you doubt the dough is moist enough, assume it isn't, and add more water. No problem if you get it too wet – just add more flour.

5   Knead for 2-3 minutes on a floured surface. As you knead, you should feel the dough getting springier as the yeast begins to work.

6   Replace the dough in the bowl, enclose in a large (preferably transparent) plastic bag and leave in a warm, draught-free place to rise to twice its size. This can be an amazing thing for children to see!

7   Punch it down gently ('knock it back') with a floury fist, re-mix the dough, then press it down evenly into your greased loaf tin.

8   Enclose the tin in the plastic bag again, leaving plenty of room around the top of the tip for the bread to rise, and put to rise again.

9   Have the oven ready at gas 8, 450°F, 225°C, and make sure you have a shelf half way up the oven to take the bread. As soon as the bread has risen into a mound above the tin, remove its bag and put in the oven. Bake for 15 minutes.

10 Then lower the heat to gas 5, 375°F, 185°C, and bake for another 35-40 minutes.

11 Tip the loaf out of the tin and put on the oven shelf upside down for 5 minutes to cook the underneath well.

12 To test: Hold the loaf upside down in an oven-gloved hand. Gently rap the bottom crust with your knuckles. If the loaf is cooked through:
    • you will hear a clear knocking sound
    • you will feel the rapping in your gloved hand! This is the ultimate test.

13 Place the cooked loaf across its tin (or on a wire rack) and leave to cool.

14 If you have any doubts, bake a few minutes longer and test again.

Eat only when completely cold – too-new bread is highly indigestible and the loaf will tear when you try to cut it. (One small compromise – you could shave off a wafer-thin end crust after an hour or so ... it will crunch like a potato crisp and be sheer heaven.)

Store, wrapped in a tea-towel, paper bag or loose plastic bag in a cool place, but not in the fridge which, surprisingly, will stale it.

This is a lot of work for one loaf. So bake four at a time (most ovens will take four on one shelf), and freeze three. It makes a tremendous financial and gourmet bargain.

BATCH BREADMAKING HINTS

When baking several loaves, make sure that:
- you bake them all on the same shelf
- the tins touch neither the sides of the oven nor each other, or the loaves will burn where metal touched metal

---

QUANTITIES FOR A SMALL LOAF:

350 g ($^3/_4$ lb) flour
200-250 ml (7-8 fl. oz) water, or more
15 g ($^1/_2$ oz) fresh yeast, OR 10g ($^1/_4$ oz) dried

Bake at gas 7, 425°F, 215°C, for 23 minutes.

FREE-FORM LOAVES

You don't have to use bread tins. Just put well-shaped mounds of dough on a greased baking sheet and bake as above.

ROLLS

1 Put ping-pong sized balls of dough on a greased baking sheet, fairly close together so they will touch and help each other to rise. Don't flatten them, as they will flatten anyway during rising.
2 Bake at gas 7, 425°F, 215°C, for 12 minutes.

IDEAS FOR BAKING BREAD WITH CHILDREN

Let children have fun kneading – don't worry if they go on too long. Don't let them nibble the raw dough, though, as uncooked yeast should not be eaten. Children could make

- rolls sprinkled with poppy or sesame seeds
- buns: add a handful of currants or sultanas, a pinch of mixed spice and a tablespoon of honey
- snails: roll out long snakes of dough, then coil round
- any solid, rounded shape: hedgehogs, mice, teddies, funny faces; use currants for features. Pinch out ears, noses and such – don't stick bits of dough on in case they drop off in baking
- gingerbread men: add a teaspoonful of powdered ginger to the recipe, a knob of butter and a teaspoon of honey. They'll be lumpier looking than with a biscuit recipe of course. If they look too strange, say they must have been wriggling about a lot in the oven.

Some features always get lost in baking, so prepare children for this. Say 'Let's see if we can make ...' rather than 'We're going to make...'

Snacks based on bread: sandwiches

Children can help with making their own sandwiches if you put out some fillings. If the fillings are moist you won't need to butter the bread first. There are lots of fillings to choose from:

- salad items of all kinds: tomato, cucumber, red, green and yellow peppers, lettuce of different types and colours, celery, radish slices, watercress, mustard and cress, spring onions, avocado, sprouted seeds such as alfalfa or chick pea
- vegetables, grated, sliced or in crunchy sticks: raw carrots, mild onion, celeriac, courgette, cooked beetroot, cooked red or white beans
- apple slices in lemon juice; mashed banana; mashed raspberries or red currants with a dusting of sugar, fresh apricots with banana slices; dried apricots, dates, raisins, sultanas
- tinned tuna, sardines, pilchards, cods roe, salmon, crab meat, prawns
- peanut butter, tahini, hummus, almond butter, hazelnut butter
- all kinds of cheese, sliced or grated; curd, cream and cottage cheese, goats' cheese, fromage frais
- cold cooked meats of all kinds
- hard-boiled and scrambled egg; slices of omelette

Put some green stuff in every sandwich to keep it moist and juicy; aim to have something crunchy too. Look at page 104 for some good combinations.

As well as slices of bread, make sandwiches with baps and rolls, French sticks and pitta bread. Experiment with a variety of bread, including cheese bread, fruit bread and dark rye.

What to put on toast?

Most of the above! You don't have to have a hot topping for toast: grilled cheese is nice, but so is a slice of cold cheese. A few other ideas:

- sardines mashed with lemon juice on shredded lettuce
- fish pâté (see recipes on page 176)

- tahini with a thin spread of honey
- grilled cheese and tomato
- herring roes: toss them in a speck of butter and add lemon juice
- olive oil – yes, just that! Worth trying
- thin layer of yeast extract (it's very salty)
- garlic toast: beat crushed garlic into butter or soft margarine
- taramasalata; try to get the sort with minimum dye
- black olive pâté (sold in jars)
- tomatoes: drain, mash, boil up to thicken somewhat; add tiny pinches of salt, pepper, cayenne and sugar
- mushrooms: toss in butter, lemon juice and black pepper (see page 150)
- baked beans mixed with shredded beetroot
- grilled fruit: (see recipe below)

FISH PÂTÉ

sardines, drained and mashed
cream cheese
lemon juice
garlic, crushed to a paste

Mix the sardines and cheese together in any proportions. Mix in a little lemon juice and garlic. Season to taste.

COD'S ROE PÂTÉ

small tin of cooked cod's roe
a knob of soft butter OR margarine
4 tsps. smatana, yogurt OR soured cream
1-2 cloves garlic, crushed to a paste
lemon juice and seasoning to taste

Beat everything together and pile on toast.

GRILLED FRUIT

1 Toast one side of a slice of bread and turn it over.
2 Cover with mashed, very ripe, tart fruit – raspberries, loganberries, stoned cherries, apricots, red currants and blackcurrants are all good.
3 Sprinkle with a little sugar and grill slowly until it caramelises.

HOT PITTA BREAD

To make a pitta bread pocket, pop the bread into a microwave oven for a few seconds, or take frozen pitta bread, run it under the cold tap then put immediately under a hot grill. The pitta should puff up slightly and become easy to slit open and fill.

PITTA POCKET

tuna
mayonnaise
cooked red beans OR sweetcorn
tomato, red pepper, lettuce

Mix some tuna and beans or sweetcorn into a little mayonnaise. Combine with two or three salad items and fill the pitta.

PERSIAN HUMMUS

500 g (1 lb) tinned or home-cooked chick peas
juice 1-2 lemons
¹/₄ jar tahini
2-3 garlic cloves crushed to a paste
1 rounded tsp. ground cumin
pinch salt and pepper

1 Drain the chick peas and rinse under the tap. Liquidise everything in enough cold water to make a completely smooth and spreadable pâté. Taste for seasoning and lemon juice as you go.
2 This looks attractive served in the traditional way in a bowl, covered with a thin layer of good olive oil, dusted with paprika and scattered with roughly chopped parsley. Eat with pitta or toast and salad.

OVEN CHIPS

Everybody likes chips – and they are nutritious apart from the amount of fat they soak up. So try these oven chips, cooked with almost no fat.

Cut scrubbed but unpeeled potatoes into 1 cm thick chips. Heat very little oil in a shallow baking tray. Toss the chips in the hot oil to coat, then bake for about 25 minutes in a hot oven, about gas 8, 450°F, 230°C, turning over once or twice.

If they're cooked enough, they should look and taste like very good conventional deep-fried chips!

KELEWELE (GHANAIAN PLANTAIN CHIPS)

2 ripe (yellow) plantains
pinch salt and pepper
oil for frying

Peel the plantains, cut into chip shapes and rub with pepper. Fry them in very hot oil until well browned and sweet.

STIR-FRIED VEGETABLE CHIPS

Stir-fry carrot, parsnip or swede chips in a small amount of oil until browned. They will caramelise and taste sweet.

POTATOES-IN-THEIR-JACKETS

An excellent and easy snack. Cut down on baking time by boiling whole potatoes until virtually done, then finish them off in a hot oven. If you've microwaved them, dry them out in an ordinary oven to improve their texture and crisp the skins.

Halve, mash, mix with something tasty and replace in the skin. Some of the following ideas are meals in themselves:

- tuna, tomato and mayonnaise
- fromage frais, yogurt or smatana
- yogurt with chopped orange segments
- yogurt mixed with diced apple, orange, chicory and Gouda cheese
- shredded ham, tongue, chicken or salami
- grated hard cheese and flaked cod
- soft herb cheese with diced cucumber
- butter or margarine with chives and sweetcorn
- butter or margarine with finely chopped, cooked Brussels sprouts, cabbage or broccoli
- chopped hard-boiled egg, mayonnaise and watercress

Garnish in some way: make a smiley face with bits of tomato or radish, perhaps with a tuft of cress for hair; or make into a boat with a half slice of orange or lemon for a sail, or 'funnels' of vegetable sticks, and float it on a sea of shredded lettuce; or strew with cheese and breadcrumbs and bubble under the grill.

POPCORN

Exciting to make while young children watch – and listen! Older children could pop their own. Fun for everyone to eat.

¹/₂ teacup of 'popping corn' – ordinary corn will not pop
1 tsp. oil
a large, heavy frying pan with a lid

1 Heat the oil in the pan, tip the pan until the oil coats the whole of the base. (Spread it with a tissue if necessary.)
2 Drop in the corn and put on the lid. After a minute or so listen to the popping noises as the grains begin to burst. When the popping stops, take off the lid and exclaim over the size and shapes of the exploded kernels.
3 Eat soon while the corn is still crisp.

LASSI

A traditional drink to have with curry, it makes a wonderful snack with a samosa or bhaji or sandwich.

Simply blend plain yogurt with water or milk and a pinch of cumin. Add, traditionally, either salt or sugar.

MIGHTY MILK SHAKE

300 ml (¹/₂ pint) fresh orange juice *2-3 drops vanilla extract*
teacupful of yogurt *1 tsp. brewers' yeast*
2-3 heaped tbl. powdered milk *1 large banana*
1 hard-boiled egg *300 ml (¹/₂ pint) milk*
grating of nutmeg *other fruit to taste*

1 Liquidise the orange juice with everything except the ½ pint milk.
2 Then blend in the milk smoothly. You can add any other fruit to taste: try raspberries for a bright pink colour. Adding part (or all) of a carton of frozen, concentrated orange juice adds sweetness and flavour without extra liquid.

A wonderful pick-me-up for children – and their parents!

THE-SLING-IN-THE-BIN LIST

We recommend that you bin – and don't re-buy – the following tooth rotters, stomach fillers and artery blockers:

- commercially prepared desserts and cakes
- commercially prepared burgers and pies
- packet mixes and toppings, etc.
- tinned fruit in syrup
- suet
- synthetic and sugared fruit drinks and squashes
- commercial 'fruit' yogurt and fromage frais
- condensed milk
- high-sugar breakfast cereals.

THE CUT-WAY-BACK LIST

And if you're buying the following more than occasionally, cut way back on:

- biscuits
- salty snacks
- mass-produced sausages
- cream, real or synthetic
- golden syrup, treacle and honey
- jam and marmalade
- concentrated fruit juices or spreads
- custard and blancmange powder

BETTER BAKING

If you are using a conventional cake or pudding recipe:

- change to wholemeal flour: actually an improvement in many cakes and puddings, particularly with chocolate recipes. Perhaps start by mixing wholemeal and white flour together and then change gradually to all wholemeal

- change to whole (i.e. 'brown') rice for puddings and such.

- change to whole semolina, and whole ('pot') barley

- cut the sugar by 50% – and cakes and puddings will taste the same! It takes courage to do this, so cut the sugar a little at a time until you've got rid of half of it. (But don't tell anyone – people taste what they expect to taste)
  However, it doesn't work with chocolate or carrot cakes unless you can add lots of dried fruit. Pity!

- In some recipes a good polyunsaturated margarine may work as well as butter; or perhaps you could use half and half. In others, such as when you are frying in butter, change to half butter and half oil, or just use oil. See if a recipe will work with less fat than stipulated

- If you're filling or decorating with cream, mix it half and half with thick yoghurt, smatana or fromage frais

- Use fresh fruit pieces for decoration and fillings

Part Three

GETTING HELP

16

MORE INFORMATION, RESOURCES AND USEFUL ADDRESSES

——— People who can help ———

Health education officer, or health promotion officer
Contact them at your nearest main hospital. They have leaflets and posters and they are keen to promote healthy eating for children. Some may be able to mount a stall at a fête or mount a display for a parents' group.

Dental health education officer, or community dental officer
Contact them at your nearest main hospital. They have leaflets and posters on healthy diets especially as they affect teeth and oral hygiene.

Environmental health officers
Contact them at your nearest town hall/county hall. They can give useful advice about kitchen hygiene, and can come and advise people who are catering for others, such as a playgroup or nursery.

And if you get food poisoning, then apart from contacting your doctor, you may want to contact the environmental health officer responsible for your area, especially if you think the food poisoning may have come from a commercial catering outlet, such as a cafe or restaurant, or even a playgroup or school.

Lastly, if you come across food that is contaminated, eg with some nasty object in it, or if you think packaged food has been tampered with, then phone your environmental health officers – they are the 'food police' in these cases.

Dietitians
Contact these through your doctor, if your child has an eating problem and would benefit from dietary advice.

Health visitors
These are specially trained nurses responsible for ensuring that all children under five are visited – usually within a few weeks of birth – and who run the baby clinics at your nearest health centre. Ask them for advice and leaflets.

—— Commercial organisations ——

Commercial companies, trade associations
Keen to give you advice and leaflets and even free samples, as soon as you ask – but remember where their main interest lies.

If you have a complaint or a suggestion for them, then here are the main babyfood companies' phone numbers (you can ask for the name and address of their customer enquiries manager):

> Milupa 0181-573 9966
> Heinz 0181-848 2632
> Farleys – now owned by Heinz
> Cow & Gate 01225-768381
> Robinsons baby foods – now owned by Cow & Gate
> Robinsons baby drinks 01603-660166
> Boots 0115-950 6111
> Sainsbury 0171-921 6000
> Safeway 0181-848 8744
> Baby Organix 0800-393511
> Wyeth 016286-4377
> Ribena 0181-560 5151

For other food companies, if your library or directory enquiries can't help then try phoning the Food and Drink Federation, 0171-836 2460.

—————— Support groups ——————

For support and advice, here are some voluntary agencies to contact:

Action Against Allergy
24-26 High Street
Hampton Hill
Middlesex TW12 1PD

Action and Information on Sugars
P O Box 459
London SE5 7EQ

Anorexic Aid
The Priory Centre
11 Priory Road
High Wycombe
Bucks
tel 01494-21431

Asthma Research Council and Asthma Society
300 Upper Street
London N1 2XX
tel 0171-226 2260

Baby Milk Action
23 St Andrews Street
Cambridge CB2 3AX
tel 01223-464420

British Diabetic Association
10 Queen Anne Street
London W1M 0BD
tel 0171-323 1531

The Child Poverty Action Group
1 Bath Street
London EC1N 9LB
tel 0171-253 3406

The Coeliac Society
P O Box 220
High Wycombe
Bucks HP11 2HY

The Eating Disorders Association
Sackville Place
44 Magdalen Street
Norwich
Norfolk NR3 1JU
tel 01603-621414

The Food Commission
3rd Floor
5-11 Worship Street
London EC2A 2BH
0171-628 7774

Foresight – the Association for Preconceptual Care
The Old Vicarage
Church Lane
Witley
Godalming
Surrey

Hyperactive Children's Support Group
59 Meadowside
Angmering
Littlehampton
W Sussex BN16 4BN

La Leche League
B M Box 3424
London WC1N 3XX
tel 0171-242 1278

Maternity Alliance
15 Brittania Street
London WC1X 9JP
0171-837 1265

National Childbirth Trust
9 Queensborough Terrace
London W2 3TB
tel 0171 221 3833

National Eczema Society
Tavistock House North
Tavistock Square
London WC1H 9SR
tel 0171-388 4097

National Society for Research into Allergy
P O Box 45
Hickley
Leicestershire
LE10 1JY
tel 01455-635212

Pre-school Playgroups Association
61 Kings Cross Road
London WC1X 9LN
tel 0171-833 0991

The Royal College of Midwives
15 Mansfield Street
London W1M 0BE
tel 0171-872 5100

School Meals Campaign
P O Box 402
London WC1 9TZ
tel 0171-383 7638

TAMBA – the Twins and Multiple Births Association
51 Thickmall Drive
Pedmoor
Stourbridge
Derbyshire
DY9 0YH
tel 01384-373642

The Vegan Society
33-35 George Street
Oxford OX1 2AY
tel 01865-722166

The Vegetarian Society
Parkdale
Dunham Road
Altrincham
Cheshire WA14 4QG
tel 0161-928 0793

The National Food Guide

The Balance of Good Health

Fruit and vegetables
Choose a wide variety

Bread, other cereals and potatoes
Eat all types and choose high fibre kinds whenever you can

Milk and dairy foods
Choose lower fat alternatives whenever you can

Meat, fish and alternatives
Choose lower fat alternatives whenever you can

Fatty and sugary foods
Try not to eat these too often, and when you do, have small amounts

Reproduced with the permission of the Health Education Authority

INDEX

additives 8, 35–7, 68, 102
allergies 12, 33, 37
  milk 24, 134
  peanut 34
  wheat 33
artificial sweeteners 68, 108
asthma 37

babies' bottles 15, 28–9
baby drinks 1, 15, 28
baby foods (commercial) 15, 18–19,
  57, 72, 109
baking with children 51, 70, 77–83,
  180
  better 181
beetroot 22, 33
behavioural disorders 28, 32, 34–5,
  37, 55, 102
birthday party food 70–1, 102–8
bran 8, 141
bread 26, 133, 171
breakfast 8, 45, 49–50, 140–2
breastfeeding 10–14, 65
  counsellors 11
brewers' yeast powder 139

calcium 6, 61
cereals (breakfast) 8, 43, 45, 50
  to make 141–2
changing eating habits 48, 181
  in pregnancy 6
chocolate (see sweets)
  caffeine in 8
citrus fruits (in weaning) 22, 33
coffee 8, 35
cola 8
coleslaw 82
colostrum 12
constipation 2, 33, 56

cows' milk (in weaning) 22, 24
crisps 3, 64, 145
cut-way-back list 182

diarrhoea 29, 34, 55
dieting 58
drinking straws 28
drinks 1, 27, 28, 34–5, 50, 55,
  64, 108
dummies 28

eating out 109
eczema 37
eggs, safety of 9, 29

fat 1, 2, 6, 8, 22, 32–3, 58, 62, 67
fibre 8, 33, 56, 61, 141
folic acid 5, 7
follow-on milks 15
food battles 56–7
food poisoning 29, 37
food refusal 40, 54, 54–9
formula milks 15
fruit drinks (imitation) 34, 55

gastro-enteritis 29, 37
grandparents 47–8

healthy eating guidelines
  for children 18–19, 67, 68, 69, 180–1
  'healthy eating plate' 191
  in pregnancy 6–9
  in weaning 22
heart disease 2, 5, 9
'herbal teas' 28
hygiene 9, 15, 29, 30
hyperactivity 34, 36, 55, 102

IQ 5
iron 8, 61, 25
  in pregnancy 5–9

jaundice 12
juice drinks 1, 15, 27–8, 33, 34, 55, 108
junk food 1, 18

La Leche League 12, 15, 188
lactose 24, 134
laxatives 33, 56
listeria 9
low birth weight 5

menus
    changing 48–50, 180–1
    planning 45, 67–8
microwave ovens 15
milk
    allergy 24
    breast-milk, value of 12–13
    follow-on milks 15
    formula milks 15
    in weaning 22, 24, 31
    lactose in 24
    tokens 16
mineral water 108
minerals 7
muesli 8
    to make 141

nuts, safety of 22, 26, 34

obesity 2, 52, 59, 62

pastry
    activities for children 78–80
    recipe 78
peanut allergy 25, 34
'pester power' 43
picky eaters 56–7, 59, 62, 134
playdough 77
pre-conceptual diet
    guidelines for 6–9
    importance of 4–6
pregnancy
    diet during 6–9
    preparing 4–6
purées, how to make 117

roughage (see fibre)
rusks 1, 21

salmonella 9, 29
salt 1, 6, 22, 32, 68
saturated fat (see fat)
sausages 49
shopping 6–9

with children 43–4
sling-in-the-bin list 180
snacks 3, 25, 32, 54–5, 68–9, 175–9
soft drinks (see drinks)
soft summer fruits (in weaning) 22, 24, 33
spices 22
spina bifida 5, 7
spinach 22, 33, 61, 97
sprouting seeds 87–9
'squash drinking syndrome' 34, 55
sugar 1, 6, 8, 22, 32, 50, 58, 62, 67–8
    in drinks 27, 28, 34–5, 55, 67
    'low-sugar' 21
swede (in weaning) 22, 33
sweeteners (artificial) 68
sweets
    how to avoid 46–8, 50–1, 62
    in chemists 19
    used as bribes 61–2

tea
    baby 'herbal' teas 28
    caffeine in 8
    for children 35
teeth 27–8, 46–7, 50, 180
    in preconceptual diet 6
tooth decay 2, 3, 28, 50
toxoplasmosis 9
treats 3, 48, 61
turnip (in weaning) 22, 33
twins, breastfeeding 15, 189

vegetables, dislike of 60–2
vitamin A 9, 61
vitamin B 5, 6
vitamin C 5, 25, 61
vitamin E 6, 61
vitamin pills 7, 37
vitamins 7, 37
    in fruits and vegetables 60

water
    in weaning 27
    mineral 27, 108

wheatgerm 25, 27
vegetarian diet in pregnancy 8
    (see also recipe section)
yogurt 27, 67
    commercial, sugar in 32, 84
    home-made 83–5

INDEX TO RECIPES

apple purée 115
apricot jelly crunch 169
avocado pear 119

baby beverage 119
baby breakfast cereal 123
baby bubble and squeak 130
baby guacamole 135
baby jacket 115
baby meatballs with dill 160
baby oatmeal 119
baby rice 114
bambino Italiano 129
banana mash 116
banana rice porridge 116
banana whizz 139
beanburgers 161
bright green cucumbers 137
brightly coloured vegetables 132
broccoli and potato cream 118
broccoli purée 117
broccoli and cauliflower purée 117
brown rice 158

carrot and lentil soup 122
carrot purée 115
cauliflower purée 117
cheese and potato cakes 135
cheese biscuits 79
cheese sables 81

cheese sauce 150
chicken liver purée 126
chicken pie 162
chicken soup 124
cod's roe pate 176
cooked fruit yogurt 131
cottage fruit 131
creamless cream sauce 149
creamy purées 115
creamy scrambled egg 142
creamy winter fruit 164
crunchy bananas 82

dairy dinner 137
dips 133

family salad dressing 156
fast fish 137
finger foods 132
first fish dinner 130
fish pâté 176
fish tasters 129
fish with cream sauce 149
fresh fruit compote 165
fresh fruit jelly: terrine des fruits 166
fresh fruit trifle 166
fresh fruit yogurt 131
fruity avocado 120
fruity potatoes 130
fruity rice porridge 114

golden apricot and banana pudding 120
golden rice for curries 159
golden sesame slices 159
grandmother Rachel's
   Polish cheesecake 170
great granola 141
green beans 120
green salad for pizza 156
grilled fruit 176

home-made bread 172
home-made burgers 160
home-made fruit yogurt 83
hot pitta bread 177
how to cook delicious fish 145
Hungarian fish casserole 148
hurry curry 158

ice-cream pudding with meringues 168
Italian tomato sauce 156

kelewele 178
kids' coffee 35
kids' coleslaw 82

lassi 179
last minute banana yogurt dessert 165
leek cream 121
leeks and green beans 121
lettuce roll-ups 81
liver, onion and apples 127
liver and tomato dinner 126
liver, leek and potato dinner 127

mackerel with apricot sauce 147
mackerel with gooseberry sauce 146
midsummer delight 138
mighty milk shake 179
mushroom sauce 150

oven chips 177

papaya 116
parsely fish cakes 136
parsley sauce 150
parsnip purée 118

pasta with bright
   red and green sauce 152
pasta with tuna 151
pastry pizzas 80
pastry snails 79
peaches and banana 120
pear purée 114
peasant pasta 152
perfect pasta 151
Persian hummus 177
Philippa's cheese balls 81
Philippa's raisin and carrot loaf 82
pizza 154
popcorn 179
porridge fit for a king 141
potatoes-in-their-jackets and fillings 178

raspberry crunch 170
root vegetable purée 118

sandwiches 175
Scottish herring 142
sesame cheese biscuits 80
soft goats' cheese with fruit 134
spaghetti bolognese 153
spicy swede and carrot 137
stir-fried vegetable chips 178
strawberry jelly ring 167
strawberry-raspberry dessert 165
super muesli 142
Swedish oat biscuits 83
sweet potato 121

tiny toddlers' breakfast cereals 142
toddlers' tea 35
tomato pie 157
trout à la meunière 144
turkey and chestnuts 128
turkey and winter vegetables 128

vegetables from the family pot 116

what to put on toast? 176
wheatgerm and milk 124
winter fruit salad 163
wolf stew 153